The Construction Project Management Success Guide

By Andreas P

Everything You Need To Know About Construction Contracts, Estimating, Planning and Scheduling, Skills to Manage Trades and Home Renovations

3rd Edition

Table of Contents

Introduction

The re-emergence of the real estate market sparked renewed optimism in construction. Across different states in the country, residential construction jobs are being undertaken in order to satisfy the demands in housing. Since residential construction projects are still a business (except when you want to build your own home), the idea is to build enough living spaces and to offer them to prospective clients or leasers at an affordable price.

Of course the success of such a goal still lies on income and the general economic outlook, but one thing is for certain: now that the housing crisis is over, more people will look forward to getting a place to call their home. There are more and more people getting into the construction industry as a means to make a living.

This widespread increase in the interest for the construction industry cannot be less perceived by the United States of America. The land of the free and opportunity, which contributes roughly ten per cent in the world's market or commercial activity, proudly ranks second in the entire planet in the list of countries with the most prominent construction market in the year 2013.

What is more, among the fifty states of the United States the city which exceeds all the rest in the country in spending their green dollars on construction is none other than the Big Apple itself – New York City. If you find these rankings a little vague enough for you to visualize and need more figures to grasp the entire picture of how huge the construction industry has become in the U.S., then allow me to present it in a different manner. Try to picture that in the year 2013 alone, the entire United States have allocated a little over six hundred and twenty seven billion U.S. dollars for the construction of structures and all these were recorded exclusively for the private industry only. This figure does not yet include all the other sectors, such as the government, the non-government units, residential and all the other sectors that have been into construction alone. To blow your mind a little harder, experts have been projecting these values to reach and even exceed a trillion U.S. dollars by the end of 2015.

Worldwide, countries with booming construction industries include those in the Europe and always topping the list of very successful construction contractors are those coming from the Republic of China. Their revenues have been reaching almost a hundred billion dollars in a year since 2013.

However, these are success stories for the big companies that have already established their names in the construction industries. Many may still be in the starting point of their construction management stages. And, I can tell you now that much like every road which leads to success that was not merely stumbled upon or not achieved by pure luck, chance of good fortune, the hard cold fact of the story lies with the truth that without expertise of scheduling this work, they may be hopelessly lost. This book is intended to help such people to ensure that they are making the most of the tradesmen that they employ and doing work in a way which is sensible not only from a cost point of view but from a work point of view.

Thank you for purchasing the book, "The Construction Project Management Success Guide: Everything You Need To Know About Construction Contracts, Estimating, Planning And Scheduling, Skills To Manage Trades And Home Renovations." This book will discuss the basic principles associated with managing the life of a construction job.

In this book, we'll talk about the Construction Project Management Life Cycle. Under this cycle, the following phases can be found:

The Initiation Phase

The Planning Phase

The Execution Phase

The Controlling Phase

The Closing Phase

Apart from the Construction Project Management Life Cycle, we'll also cover contracting and contract management, the participants in the construction job, the existing building code, self-managing a construction project, and the critical success factors in every contracting job.

This book is written for both Project Managers and homeowners who wish to build residential properties; hence the concepts discussed herein are general but are important just the same when it comes to approaching the construction process.

Thank you again for buying this book. I hope you will learn a lot from it. A contractor should use it as a standard for all construction of private homes or by an independent company because there is an order in which you need to do this work to maximize on profits but also to provide homes which are up to code and which comply with all regulations.

This book will act as a guide and will walk you through all the necessary work orders and supervision that is needed to make sure your jobs are carried out in a timely manner and that you also make the most of the contractors time, so that time is not wasted on site, between stages. This is one of the biggest problems for building management and if you organize things on a proper scheduled basis, you won't have to deal with this complication.

I have written the book in easy to understand language so that you can make the most of all of the information contained herein to get your workload sorted out in such a way as to maximize profit and the use of your tradesmen. It will also show you that discounts do not always mean cutting corners. They just mean that regular supplies can be obtained at cheaper prices if your supplier is notified of your intention of bulk buying. This is covered in detail and the amount of savings that you can make by doing this is vast. Look at the property twins on the TV, and their slickness and what you are actually seeing is construction organization at its best because these guys have done just that – getting great discounts on products they need for many jobs. You too can capitalize on this.

Read on and you will see there is a great way of handling construction contracts with your contractors and with suppliers, to keep your jobs running smoothly providing many people with the news homes that they have been seeking. The property industry is vast and sometimes a little baffling and this book breaks it down into easily digestible parts so that you are no longer left wondering about any aspect of renovation.

It is hoped that you will keep this as your handbook and that it will help you through the difficulties of the construction industry's maze of codes and legal requirements as well as help you to organize work in a timely and cost effective manner.

Chapter 1: Equipping you with all the Basics to Get You Started with Understanding Construction Project Management

Chapter Objectives:

**Some Useful Words in Construction Project Management You Need to Know

**What is a Construction Project Management?

**What are Construction Project Managements for?

**Overview on the Structured Multiple Phases of Construction Project Management

In order for a construction project management to be capable of producing, if not already producing, an intended result with a striking effect, then the entire project venture should have a systematic and well-thought of plan of action. These plans for attaining the specific project goals should always be kept in the minds of everyone involved in the project, so as not to lose focus and be swept off track. When a concrete, elaborate plan has been hatched then the implementation of these plans would always require tools that will ensure the smooth operation and follow through of the design. The construction project management team should always consider the expectations of their clients; the project should be proceeding in a manner that is approvable to the client.

The completion of a successful project means the proper carrying out of the set rules in management that has direct or indirect control over modifications in the fundamental elements such as budget, time, resources, range, and risk. The control over these aspects is often flexible, where modifications are welcome as the need arises, and often in favor of attaining maximum efficiency and making the most out of the current situation at hand.

It would be wise for stakeholders to consider project management in construction with the utmost care, prudence and good judgment as this step is often the most critical one in construction. If at or near the beginning of the project, the stakeholder has invested reasonably into the preparation, programming and designing of the project then the company has saved themselves the possible headaches due to occasional, unintentional and definitely unwanted delays and additional costs.

Most modern companies have seen the significance and difference that an efficiently carried out construction project management have done and are now more than willing to allot a little extra budget on project management rather than on post construction "fix ups or retouches". In order to understand more about the characteristics that would qualify for a good construction project management, let us first provide you with better understanding of the big picture concerning the topic; everything basic you need to know; the terms that would help you understand project management better and some pointers on the use and purpose of construction project management.

Some Useful Words in Construction Project Management You Need to Know

Construction management (CM) or Construction Project Management (CPMA) refers to the entire process of the construction project starting from the act of formulating it, to the skillful and effective regulation of important concepts and characters integrated into the project and control seeing that the project reaches until its final stage of completion.

Programme management (ProgM) had something to do with taking charge of the case of the client.

Project Control (PC) pertains to the monitoring and giving account of the improvements and progression of the project in terms of its cost, time and quality. What makes this different from construction project management (CPM) is that CPM is characterized by being more influential which produces certain change or effect while PC is more inactive and less subject to change and variability.

Project Leader (PL) is the individual who behaves as the manager and is held accountable for making sure that the objectives of the project are met. (More details on the role of the project leader in the following chapters of this book)

Project director (PD) is the person who guides and supervises the operations of a big project composed of many smaller sub categories. This person may also be in charge of a project management system.

Owner representative (OR) I is the advocate who takes the place of the proprietor of the project. This assignment may either be made by the company internally or externally.

Document Control (DC) is the fundamental purpose in the list of responsibilities of the project manager.

Build Operate Transfer (BOT) or Build Own Operate Transfer (BOOT) is a kind of activity done to fund the project in which a private company obtains a contract coming from the public or private sector granting the right to operate a subsidiary business. Matters included in this agreed contract involves details on the source and allocation of funds, planning, innovation, conception and operation of the project as stated in the binding agreement.

Private Finance Initiative (PFI) is the financial backing of public basic facilities by a private source in order to forge partnerships among the public and private sectors

Joint Venture (JV) refers to the act where at least two companies either from similar or dissimilar settings and interests work jointly in order to see the successful finishing of a mutual project. This partnership does not always divide the shares of control over the project equally; more often than not a principal contractor will under normal conditions be able to place a bigger bet on decisions concerning the project due to a higher share in the business deal.

Guaranteed Maximum Price (GMP) denotes the maximum or greatest possible amount of the cost of the project. This detail is stated and emphasized in the yielded contract.

Multiple Prime Contract (MPC) is simply the literal definition of the phrase where a binding agreement is made between one or more contractors under separate contracts to carry out a particular set of function that are under the same project. This condition may be done whether the two contractors should function in a consecutive manner during the course of the project development or happening at the same time.

What is a Construction Project Management

First of all, recall the definition of a project in order to better understand its function. A project is simply a set of work activities that is reciprocally connected and are consistently kept in check to ensure that activities and progress in the work are in line with a specific agreed upon schedule, scope and budget. The end goal of the project is to be able to carry out and perform actions that lead to the accomplishment of goals set by the company. All this construction project management is legally bound by a contract agreed upon and must always have a commencement and a culmination.

When it comes to the determination of the essential quality of a construction project, one needs to consider its three important fundamental characteristics: the budget, the scope and the project's time-frame or schedule.

First of all, the budget is an essential life source for any project. It is this factor that predetermines the scope and the time frame of the project. It is also the biggest constraining factor since a number of restrictions are often encountered when a project is limited by resources in funding. Budget can be first predetermined through a rough estimate done in the preliminary stages of the project. This very rough estimate can then be refined further to give a closer monetary value to the clients and project constituents during analysis and studies conducted in the development of design stages. This is included in the engineering phase of project management, which we will understand further in the section of this book where I present to you the complete life cycle of a construction project.

Next characteristic is the scope of the project which gives every project their unique signature identity. The scope should always be presented as written and includes elaborate information on the requirements pertaining to the series of processes involved and to be conducted in the project, the degree or relative position of service, the deliverables or products expected as outputs during the course of the project, restriction requirements as mandated by the region rules, principles or laws and the grade of excellence of the entire project.

The scope is an active characteristic of any project and undergoes numerous changes as novel information is collected during the course of the project. It is necessary that the scope of the project be in constant refinement to ensure the quality of excellence of the work.

And finally, a project with a clear scope and determined budget should be defined with a start and a finish. This characteristic is outlaid by the time frame or schedule of the project. The project plan produced at the initial phases should indicate when it is projected to start and must contain the end date when the construction is expected to finish. The scope must first be designed in accordance with the agreed upon budget and then the schedule determined as patterned to this essential information. Whenever setting up the schedule, managers should always make sure that time frames are practical and are attainable. The time table should include activities that are capable of being accomplished in the given amount of time and should never be under estimated and at the same time over estimated. Activities should be estimated with time duration and arranged in a reasonable order and chronological succession.

What Construction Project Managements are for: Its Principles and Objectives

Construction project management is by and large used by the private or public sector in order to carry through a project where outputs provided as products of development can cope with requirements stated in the scope of the project and always within the means and limitations of the budget and time frame agreed upon and provided for. These actions should all be in line with satisfactory quality, and done ensured under acceptable security degree, safety and risk.

Construction management serves to determine the essential quality of the aims and plans of the project which include but are not only limited to the following: budget, scope, time frame, evaluation of performance expectations, and recruitment of participants or contributors for the project.

Another function of the project management is to ensure that resources are utilized as efficiently as is possible and reasonable. Resources are used in a manner that the project is able to make the most out of it without compromising quality output. These resources include equipment and materials, as well as human labor.

The act of accomplishing specified aim or executing activities in the project with the most effective use of labor and time coordination. And also the power to direct or determine the course of the project including the designing, planning, estimating, making contracts and the construction proper itself is a primary and fundamental responsibility included in the construction management.

And finally, the troubleshooting of problems encountered during the course of the completion of the project as well as resolving of conflicts is one function of project managements. Construction project management is also an effective tool in book keeping details during the implementation stage as well as efficient documentation of everything that has been done from start to finish of the project. This information can prove to be highly useful as references for up and coming projects.

Project management should be able to handle the demands and requirements of the clients on top of the restraints that are inherent to the project itself. And the proper management of these demands involve being able to deal with them by providing the best scenario for scope, budget and time frame that does not depreciate the quality of the deliverables or compromise the caliber of the project.

Whenever dealing with the attainment of the objectives of a certain project, the biggest challenge and hurdle often comes from unexpected "additions" and changes to the original scope of the project. Take for example the sudden change in the demand of the user; right in the middle of construction would such as sudden extension of a building under construction or the modification of its internal framework or addition of internal structures, and the like. This modification request that happened without warning and in a considerably short space of time might require the project to take a totally different mode of action entirely. It is in these scenarios where having a clean and distinct outline of the project's schedule of activities and details of procedures come to serve a very useful function. Having an efficient and systematic project management will allow for these modifications with little, or quite possibly no, trouble. Procedures can be redirected or added in order to at a greater degree or extent continue to meet the urgent request of the client.

Overview on the Structured Multiple Phases of Construction Project Management

The structured five basic phases of construction project management includes the initiating, planning, executing, monitoring and controlling and finally the closing. Details on each of these phases are properly described in individual chapters included in this book but for the sake of giving you an introductory sampler on what exactly you should expect yourself to get into, allow me to present a simple overview of these phases in this chapter. Allow me as well to present the roles each phase plays in the goals of project management of constructions.

In the initial phase, the conception of the project is often being done where an approximate calculation of the value of a project will be examined very carefully and considered with utmost attention to details. It is at this phase that the project will be assessed and analyzed if it would indeed prove to be beneficial to the organization or not. In a simultaneous manner, a team will be created to determine the practical attainability of the project.

The second phase that comes next to the initiating phase is the planning phase. It is in this basic phase where the project is defined further. This is where project plans as well as the very crucial project scope is determined and may possibly be put into documentation. After determining the feasibility of the project during the initiating phase, the schedule of activities to be done will then be outlined in this second phase of the project. At this stage of the project, there should be a dedicated team that is focused solely on this project and details involving its budget calculation, estimation and analysis, as well as the creation of a time frame of activities to be performed and the list of resources that will be used in the project.

Upon finishing up on the planning phase of the project, by then the team should have more or less a concrete picture of how the project should proceed and progress. The next phase that should follow planning would be the execution phase. It is in this stage that the project is officially launched into motion. Schedule of tasks and activities are spread throughout teams or individuals designated and each cooperative unit are briefed and imparted with their specific tasks and duties.

The controlling phase which follows the launch of the project is, to put it quite simply, the evaluation and monitoring stage where assigned leaders and project managers will be going over teams and individuals in charge as well as product outputs to check the progress of the project. To see if the deliverables meet the standards and deadlines stated in the actual plan and if the project status is at a favorable position. It is in this stage where project performance is appraised for extent, quality and ability to cope with client demand of scope, budget and resource. The project leaders may have to alter or regulate the resources available as well as the time frame or whatever seems necessary in order to prevent the project from falling behind expectations.

The final and last phase of construction project management is the closing. This phase is necessary to make sure that contract agreed upon in the starting phase of the project is indeed followed. The closing phase comes after all the tasks indicated in the project plan have been finished and the user or stakeholder has given approval to the output and judged it to be satisfactory or commendable. A final evaluation is required in order to indicate and point out the project's weak points as well as the strong points. These evaluation scores would provide future activities to learn from the project's record.

Chapter 2: The Critical Success Factors in Construction Project Management

Chapter Objectives:

**The Critical Success Factors for Construction Project Management

**The Core Qualities of a Project Manager

**The People Involved with the Construction Project

By 2016, the world will probably behold the greenest residential complex ever built in the world: the Clearpoint Residences. A high-rise apartment building with 46 stories, Clearpoint Residences will feature huge gardens to regulate temperature and will use solar panels to generate electricity.

No, the building is not currently anywhere in the United States but in a place near Colombo, Sri Lanka. When the building is complete, the world will not only see a success in residential property construction but also an innovation towards greener Earth. What makes a construction project successful to achieve such feats?

Note that the first chapters of this book will provide you with fundamental information and key lessons for self-managing a construction project. Take time and welcome these lessons from the initiation phase to the closing phase. Remember that acquiring the skills necessary for construction project management cannot be rushed. In this day and age, people are becoming more conscious of economically viable types of housing because it isn't just today that counts any more. It's the housing of tomorrow that will give families a future that won't cost them more than they have put into the initial home. Green style building is taking off all over the world and you need be aware of it to keep up with the competition, the standards and the innovations, which are coming onto the market all the time.

The Critical Success Factors for Construction Project Management

The industry of construction is characterized by being constantly ever changing, always with something new and different every now and then and never at a state of stationary condition. This dynamic quality of construction industry may be attributed in part to the racing unpredictability of technology, the fluctuation of prices for resources at any given time as well as the variability of budgets for the projects and the courses of action of the project as it undergoes growth and improvement. During the early days of the construction industry, the building of infrastructures was in a relative manner unmistakably simple. But in these times of the highly advanced science and technology as well as society and economy, construction projects have become more complicated and most often require input of considerable physical and mental effort in order to accomplish the construction. It did not take long for the construction project management to become a topic being given careful consideration to. In order to increase the effectivity of any construction project, Critical Success Factors or CSFs are now being taken cared of with extreme caution, prudence and tact.

The expression CSFs used in the language of the proper project management has been around for only a little over three decades and in fact was first used in the year 1982 by Rockart. The definition of Critical Success Factors in construction is quite literally anything that contributes causally and results in the success of the project whether it may be directly or indirectly. Critical Success Factors are prominent attributes or aspects, distinguishing qualities, conditions or variables that once introduced into construction project management may promote a substantial effect on the success of the project if sustained in the right manner.

Currently, experts and researchers have not yet agreed upon an exact set of CSFs that can be applied universally in project management. A different study may suggest a different set of CSFs while another similar study may present a totally different list. The reason behind this lack of agreement can be attributed to the yet undefined reference point for a successful project (and the factors that influence it) by which other projects can be evaluated against.

Many popular reviews and research articles have categorized Critical Success Factors (CSFs) into five main categories. This categorization is based upon the critical appraisals of previously published literatures dedicated for the management of projects, the practices involved in this management, the aims and goals included in each project management, the carrying into action and execution of the project.

The five main categories suggested to evaluate the work conducted in the project are: Project Management Action, Project Procedures, Human Related Factors, External Environment Issues and Project Related factors. These five categories will be defined and differentiated in detail in the next texts:

- *The Project Management Action*: Many experts have considered that this categorical factor of success is crucial for the success of the project in the entirety. Tools for management can enable the project manager to plan and carry out their construction and also to increase the prospects of the project for success.

  This particular category concentrates mostly on the system of communication, the efforts done during planning, the development of an appropriate structure in the project management administration, the implementation of an effectual plan for safety, the implementation of a good and reliable plan for quality control and assurance and the management of some other team member's works.

  All these details under the project management factors for success should have sufficient communication within and outside of the project team circle, should have proper technical aspects for control, should have capabilities for critical assessment or suggestions to improve performance among the team, should have the ability to troubleshoot and solve problems if they do arise, should have effective coordination, should have effective decision making capacity, should have properly scheduled checkups on the progress and resources of the project, should have good project organization structure where the progress is faithful to the plan and time frame constructed and should have well enough research on management histories related to the current project at hand.

- **Project Procedures** – this factor includes the act of acquiring and getting possession of resources for the project as well as the bidding methods or auctioning involved in the project and the elaborate and systematic plans of action involved in such deals.

This category can also be referred to as "Procurement Related Factors". This is the underlying structure upon which construction has been anchored on, come to be and is incurred. Two major traits can be used to measure this factor and they are the method of procurement where the organization is selected to plan, design and start with construction of the project, and the second trait is the method of tendering which is the set of sequence steps utilized for picking out of the members of the project team.

- **Human Related Factors** – These human factors constitute the involvement or participation of the client in past projects and their background on construction, the essential characteristics of the client, how big the organization of the client is, the demands of the client with regards to preference on budgeting for the construction, time frame agreeable to both parties, and the quality of the client if they would go so far as taking part in the decision making

21

of the project, the defining of functions for members, contributing to the layout of the project as well as the construction proper.

Also referred to as the Project Participants Related Factors, the Human Related Factors consider the human resources as the central recipe for the project management and are essential for the construction to start, operate and finish. These important roles include the contractor, client, consultants, project manager, subcontractor, manufacturers and suppliers. The client as well as the representative of the client both plays crucial roles in the rate of how fast construction proceeds.

Apart from the client, players who take part in handling larger responsibilities in the project management are the designers. Designers are very important in construction project management because they are involved in the construction from the initiation phase up to the closing and completion part of the project. Factors that need to be monitored for successful and efficient work performance of designers include experience of the design team in completion of related projects, the intricateness of the project, as well as the delays and errors that go hand in hand with production of the documents for design

The moment the project reaches the construction stage, it is then that the main contractor along with the other subcontractors involved start with their principal obligations. Details that determine the success of this factor for the main contractor and his or her subcontractors are the level of experience that the contractor has with construction project management, his or her ability to manage the project on site, the main contractor's degree of participation in supervising and subcontracting, the excess of cash revenues over cash outlays of the contractor, his or her efficiency in controlling the project's budget and cost and lastly the contractor and subcontractors' rapidity in disseminating information within and out of the project team.

- **External Environmental Issues** – For this critical success factor, issues such as social, economic, political, physical and sudden technology advancements are emphasized. Many researchers attribute the success of any business venture, or in our case construction, to the environmental factor. Environment used in this context could refer to any or all extraneous influences on the construction process

- *Project Related Factors* – This critical success factor center around the type of project, the fundamentals and basic attribute of the project as well as how big the project is. The scope of the project is hypothesized as a useful indicator of how fast you can expect construction to finish. In order to measure the progress and status of the project related factors, measure the type of project, the essential attributes of the project, and number of floors of the project.

Another method of categorizing Critical Success Factors in construction may be to divide it into three broad categories: economic, ecological or environmental, and social or communal. These factors may include as part of something broader a number of other constituents which needs to be operating in unison to ensure that the project is finished right on time. For the moment, however, let us now focus on these three CSFs. See the descriptions below.

- **Economic** - a residential structure should be cost-efficient throughout its lifespan.

- **Ecological** - a residential structure should be efficient when it comes to waste management, irrigation, energy, and materials.

- **Social** - a residential structure should be safe, comfortable, and flexible with respect to the different kinds of people who'll live in it.

The essential qualities or characteristics by which construction is naturally built upon, is full of risks and uncertainties. Firms or systems of committees offering construction project management in the industry do not always make certain that the outcome of the project would be a hundred per cent fail proof. This is true even for big organizations that have established their names in the construction industry. We can say this with much confidence because the success of any construction project depends heavily on how well and efficiently the project was controlled and managed during the duration of its implementation. When it comes to looking for support in matters of making a decision for the project, the critical success factors (CSFs) may prove to be highly useful.

The determination of the critical success factors will give any firm, company or organization a fighting advantage and is the primary core of success whenever dealing with project management. It is important for anyone dealing with construction project management to have his fair knowledge of the critical success factors. The CSFs can bring about a return of satisfied clients, professional individuals seeking for a position in your company and inevitably prosperity and reputation will follow.

If the three categories above seem impossible to achieve all the same time, wait until you read about the specific factors that construction teams can contribute towards its attainment. Listed below are the 3 major factors that construction project management should have:

- **Competent construction team** –Competent construction project management is rendered useless without a competent team. The selection of people you hire for your project can dictate its outcome. With that in mind, be sure to get people who can keep up in terms of standards. There are contractors who have learned the new ways of constructing with materials

24

that are considered "green" and it's worthwhile getting in touch to find out the different services that they offer. People want value but they don't mind paying a little more initially for it if it eventually gives them the comfort and shelter that is promised by "Earth friendly" construction that also takes into account the economical running of a home.

- **Authority exercised by the Project or Construction Manager** – The roles and responsibilities of the project manager will be elaborated throughout this book. Pay close attention to the fundamental skills required in a project manager for greater success. If you're reading this book, then there is a good chance that *you* will be taking one of these crucial positions. If this is the case, learn hard and work even harder. A project manager needs to understand all of the processes that will go on during the building of a home. It's not enough to actually blame a contractor for not working up to the expected quality. You need to have checked their quality on former jobs and to know that they can deliver exactly what it is that you need and do it on time.

- **Understanding of the construction project** – In construction, you can't afford the ignorance of even one member in your team. In assembling a competent construction team, make sure they are duly briefed to acquire an understanding of the entire project. The way plans (design and specs) are laid out and presented will also have an impact on this. They also need to know time schedules because this will affect whether they are available to do the work in hand. Thus, as a project manager, you need to know that first, and then tie them down to a standard and a timescale in which to work. If you are in doubt as to whether they can meet your timescales, look elsewhere. I found that having a bit of background on people helps considerably, such as talking to people who have had work done by subcontractors. One tip is to see whether the firm employ their own workers or whether they use subcontractors who are varied depending on who is available. In the latter case, you need to know that they can vouch for the work of subcontractors and be sure that they can come up to the standards set on the particular job. Subcontracting is a little risky since you will get who is available, rather than who has the expertise. It is far better to work with companies who employ their own workforce because they can give guarantees as to the standard of work and you will be able to approach them or hold retentions of payments until that work is to your satisfaction.

Other than the three given above, here are additional factors to consider for construction project management. Note that some of these are only for large-scale construction projects and are inapplicable for residential constructions/renovations.

Support from the top management or the stakeholders

On a larger housing project where finance is coming from stakeholders or top management, you need to be able to rely upon the different stage payments to make sure that your contractors are paid on time. You also need them to explain the scope of the housing project and the timescales when land is made available for building works. Liaise with the stakeholders and make sure that you are working on the same lines as they are and that you have the same vision.

Involvement of the stakeholders

Stakeholders may not be practical workers, but you may be able to enlist their help on the project to get your supplies at reasonable costs, thus keeping the price of the project on track. The stakeholders may also be interested in helping with the initial layout of projects, as they will feel that they are contributing. The more people you have involved, the more the flow of ideas. If they want to be involved, use them for research of different methods of building that may be being implemented in your area and finding out about any housing grants that may be applicable to the particular housing project. For example, if constructing homes for the elderly, you need very clear guidelines on what is expected such as door widths to take wheelchairs etc., and there may be government help for this sector of society. Let the stakeholders do the running around on this kind of information, as it will really save you time.

Realistic cost projection and time estimates

Many contractors make promises about timescales and give estimations of what things will cost. You need these to be realistic. If you are working on renovations this is particularly relevant because so many things get uncovered during the course of a job that may not have been figured into the calculations. Always have a 35 per cent contingency fund to cover these unforeseen extras and make sure that you know as soon as problems are likely to occur. If a tradesman has given you a definite quotation to work within a definite time scale, find out if he is prepared to sign a contract with a late completion clause, which will significantly reduce the price of the work if not finished on time. A good quality contractor will be happy to sign this because they are prepared to put their money where their mouth is. That's important.

The trouble is that each trade depends upon the dates set for completion of one part of the project before the next stage can be done. This means that the time schedules of different workers have to be tallied in together, so that there is a smooth movement between each of the stages of building. You don't want to be waiting for an electrician to finish his work, so that the decorator can begin his or have contractors on site who are waiting to do their work because someone else is off schedule. It all costs you money and that's something you cannot afford to throw away at this stage of the game.

Your time estimates also have to take into account inclement weather as this may delay certain work from being performed. Make sure that you know the whole story because every day of ownership of a house that is left unsold or unfinished costs you or your company money.

Proper communication and information dissemination

So many housing projects go amiss because of miscommunication. When you have proper plans in place which are architecturally sound and which have been passed by the planning department, there should be no deviation from these plans as these can cost you time and money to rectify, especially if the planning department find your workers have cut corners or have not worked to the measurements given. Liaising with contractors on a daily basis is necessary for this very purpose but you need to be informative and friendly without making the workers feel stifled. Once you are sure that the workers understand all that is being asked for them and have the right schematics for their part of the job, you can leave them to it, inspecting only when it's necessary.

You will need a schematic for your plumbers, septic tank installation (if applicable), the building itself, the roof, the electrical system and the kitchen installation, plus having diagrams of bathrooms and shower rooms so that there is no question as to where plumbing needs to be made allowance for or where electricians are required to do the initial preparation for the home. Remember that if you are installing under floor heating and solar panels, these need to be worked out in advance so that time is not wasted.

Ownership of the project by those involved

In many schemes, owners of the project get involved in the work that you do. In a case such as this, they need your assurance that everything is on track. If you are working for a client who is asking you to build their home for them, expect them to be curious at every step along the way. However, you also need to let them know at the agreement of the planning department that further changes will cost extra money and that it is preferable if they agree all works that they want to be done initially. This can save a lot of time and give them that sense of ownership that they need. Explain that changes to the plans at a later date can mean a lot of additional work and adjustment to many contracts that you have with contractors and that you prefer to take time agreeing on all of their requirements in advance to save this from happening.

Some owners are happy to leave you to the job, though it is more frequent that these people want to see what their workforce are doing at any one particular time and may call by to see what the progress is. They will be keep to have the keys to their home so you need to have time schedules that will not disappoint or be sure to let them know if you think that the contract will run over the allotted time, so that they can make their removal arrangements fit in with the work that you have to perform.

Performance monitoring and ongoing feedback

It will be your job as project manager to make sure that everything is running according to schedule and to adjust those schedules when things happen, keeping the job running on time by being able to make savings in other areas of the work. Because of this responsibility, it's important to keep on top of the job and to know if there are problems, which are likely to slow down the process.

Strategic planning and control

Project management includes so many different aspects that you may not have been aware of when you took on the job. You need to plan for one set of contractors to finish when the other is ready to start. Wasted time between them means that no work is actually being performed on site and that's costly. Your strategic planning and control is vital to the work being done on time. You can't have tilers waiting to tile when others have not finished their stage of the work and the walls are not free to be tiled. The order of work is vital to this part of the job that you do, so have a chart showing exact timings and make sure that all the workers are on time – or that those not yet started know that there is going to be a delay if problems occur. It's your job to keep everyone advised. Yes, that means spending a lot of time on the phone to suppliers and tradesmen. Late delivery of items to the site can hold things up considerably. Having carpenters on site to put together a kitchen that hasn't arrived costs money. Make sure that there is alternative work that they can be doing until the kitchen arrives.

Strategic risk management

This means being aware of all risks and having the insurance to cover those risks. Your workforce is going to be working with all kinds of hazardous conditions and materials. You also need to know at certain points during the contract if you can risk jumping ahead or if you can use laborers who are less costly to perform certain laborious tasks to move the project on.

Project team problem solving skills

When you are on site, there will be problems. Expect them and be ready to help solve them. When you work in an environment where things are changing daily, the progress or delay of that work can be due to problems that you need to solve. Be prepared to be there and to solve them, so that the workforce is not hampered by misunderstanding of drawings or being supplied with the wrong supplies. That's your job and if this goes smoothly, your workforce will be a lot happier to have you onboard looking after their interests.

It looks like a lot, but remember that a lot of people or participants are involved in a construction project. On top of the team is the Project Manager who reports to the management or the stakeholders. Does this mean that a homeowner who wishes to oversee the building of his own house cannot be a Project Manager? He can, but the knowledge brought in by an experienced Project Manager is more beneficial if the goals of construction are to be achieved. In effect, the homeowner becomes a stakeholder and the management will be those to whom the construction team reports.

Remember that another purpose of this book is to allow you to *self-manage* a residential construction or home renovation. In other words, you should be able to gain sufficient knowledge to qualify for construction project management *by the end of all chapters.* In other words, it is recommended NOT to start any construction project prior to completing this book. The entire process requires you to learn crucial knowledge and skills through all the phases of construction.

Understanding the Responsibilities of the Project Manager

The Project Manager has the most important responsibility of formulating a program for a definite course of action for the construction at hand. The Project Manager should then make sure that he or she is able to watch over the project and direct its course of action until the project has seen completion.

The minimum requirements for a person to be a Project Manager is in most cases an associate's degree, some may even require a completed degree in engineering with at least four years of formal studies and five years or so of experience in a related field. There is strictness in the screening of Project Managers because his or her responsibilities in the construction project management are not something that could be taken lightly. Not taking the construction seriously may result to wasted time, money and efforts of every member who dedicated his or her investments for the project. Best case scenario is the Project

Manager may be able to pull it off because the building did not fall apart and the project manager has been congratulated for a job well done. Worst case scenario is the building constructed was not able to hold itself up and most of the materials used for the building fell apart because the Project Manager for the construction was not able to carefully plan out and oversee the construction. This mistake may seem simple and of course unintentional, but may lead to injuries for people or even death. It is therefore very important that the Project Manager knows and commits to execute his or her responsibilities with utter devotion and commitment to some purpose.

To clarify, an individual who is skilled in construction can become the Project Manager when building his own home but he may still have to work with construction companies to help him through the different phases in construction. Further, the role of the Project Manager can be described as follows:

- The Project Manager goes through the proposal and determines when and how work will be performed. Before the start of the construction, the Project Manager must devise a design in a systematic manner indicating the plan for the project and detailing what he or she and his or her team will in actual fact be doing. This going over of the proposed project also includes preparatory work that is required and must be attended to and completed before the start of the construction.

- The Project Manager is responsible for accomplishing a budget or cost estimate of the entire project. This stage of the project is very crucial because it determines the monetary value at which the company of the Project Manager will propose an amount in return for its services.

- The Project Manager is a supervisor who not only makes sure that construction is progressive, but also makes sure that he is responsible for those who do the work.

- The Project Manager formulates an organized list of project expected outputs in order to provide the team with a useful guide that each member of the team must be faithful to in order to make sure that the work is completed in the most time-efficient and cost-effective way possible. And also to save the team members from having to put in unnecessary efforts.

- The Project Manager is responsible for procurement and ensures that all of the people involved in the construction process are equipped with the proper tools. The personnel that the Project Manager directs and supervises would not be able to fulfill their function without the proper set of tools and equipment. No matter how industrious the work force of the project team is, without the right instrument to accomplish the goals of the project, these people would be next to useless. It is therefore important that the project team find a way to take extra care of their equipment and tools so that the budget would not be compromised. The Project Manager may choose to assign a head or designate himself or herself for the task of ensuring the proper storage, and timely inventory of these materials. The careful use and handling of tools and equipment will not only keep the cost for purchase of these materials at a minimum but time would not be unnecessarily expended due to possible delays caused by repairs of equipment or purchasing of new tools.

- The Project Manager is responsible in setting specific goals in reference to the contract. He sets performance conditions and turns in deliverables to ensure that the terms in the contract are slowly being fulfilled.

It may be true that it is not the job of the Project Manager to do manual labor in construction, but he or she holds the responsibility of making sure everything stated in the signed contract is accomplished accordingly, within the time restraints and not exceeding the proposed budget for the project. After the client signs the contract and agrees upon the designed project proposal, the Project Manager as a rule establish specific goals that needed to be met in order to live up to the contract. It is the setting up of these specific goals that the Project Manager applies efficient use of micro managing skills.

- The Project Manager ensures that the project or work components are completed on time. He is also responsible in reviewing each day's accomplishments to ascertain the progress of the construction job.

The contract signed by the client before the start of construction, more often than not includes sanctions that require the project constructors to pay back a certain amount to the client in the instance that construction was not able to meet the agreed upon deadline. The Project Manager, therefore, should always keep time management a top priority during the entire course of the project from phases of pre-construction to post construction.

- The Project Manager makes it a point that the construction process does not exceed the budget. Before construction starts, costs are projected. This aspect of the responsibilities of Project Managers is of extreme importance in construction project management because it almost conclusively fixes the framework from where the project will be rooted on as well as the possible savings that can be obtained after construction. While there may be overruns, it will still be the Project Manager's responsibility to operate within such costs. This function is very similar to the concept of Value Engineering.

- The Project Manager is the key point in communication. He communicates with his bosses and the client on a regular basis to discuss milestones, challenges, and needs. During construction, everyone in the site looks up to the Project Manager as the supervisor in everything. However, the truth is the Project Manager also works under two supervisors to whom he or she must constantly answer to.

It is the job of the Project Manager to update the company of the construction project management under which he or she serves, and at the same time it is also his or her job to always keep the client who requested the construction well informed with the progress of the project.

- The Project Manager is the person who exercises the priority control in the construction site. The Project Manager gets to supervise the entire team in the construction site and makes sure that the plans he or she designed gets done and successfully completed by the hard hats composing his or her team. This human resource management involves bringing order and organization as well as commanding with authority the efforts of the workers in the construction site.

- The Project Manager acts as the boss when it comes to ensuring that proper and correct work is done and has an important involvement in the selection for hire of personnel who will work through these work goals in the project team. Along with the selection, the improvement of the strengths, skills and work attitudes of the workers falls upon the project manager. If the project manager is responsible for the hiring of the work force of the project team, it also means that the project manager has the power to dismiss and let go of employees who are not able to meet and conduct the requirements they are expected to fulfill.

- The Project Manager is the point person when it comes to dispute resolution. Not all construction jobs are completed without a bit of a fuss, so the Project Manager has to address such problems whether it is related to workers, equipment, budget, and so on.

Whenever faced with having to deal with disagreements in the work place, the best way to resolve this is to immediately severe the dispute right from where it originated. The Project Manager must therefore learn to be able to discern possible rousing of problems, must have readily apparent means to keep these unhealthy situations from arising and also must have solutions handy that will effectively bring these often times inevitable disputes to an end without seriously causing a threat to the progress of the project. Remember again that for construction project management, time is of crucial importance so the project cannot afford to lose time, and probably resources, just because individuals involved in the project cannot find it in themselves to get along for the sake of the project.

These disputes are not only for workers in the construction field, but Project Managers may also occasionally find themselves at reverse ends of the table with their clients. These situations are close to impossible to avoid because of the stressful nature of constructions. The project is always pressed with stress due to demands for deadlines, fund limitations, excellent performance and at times misunderstandings caused by poor communication. The best way to handle these kinds of disagreements is to deal with it very carefully in order to make sure that the relationship with the client is kept at amicable terms during the duration of the project from start to finish. This is when the Project Manager is expected to deal with the problem as soon as able and if possible through an unofficial setting, the Program Manager must do everything necessary and in good order just to avoid stalling the project.

- The Project Manager drafts the contract between the construction company and the client. This is done in consideration with the client's requirements alongside the results of scoping and cost estimates. This contract more often than not includes all the details of the job at hand and it would just be right that the Project Manager be connected by participation in the crafting of this said contract. During the drafting of the contract, it would be best for the Project Manager to acquaint himself or herself with the targets and demands cited in the agreement; this would serve as a huge advantage during the start of construction where the Project Manager starts setting up specific goals to be met by the team.

The Project Manager must also be present in all contract signing under the same project. Contracts among other subcontractors, suppliers and architects must be involved in the deals made with everything and everyone that has anything to do with the project.

- Finally, the Project Manager is responsible in managing risks. There will be challenges in every construction job, and the Project Manager is there to make sure that risks are minimized and that the impact of such risks does not bring the entire construction work down.

In order for the project to avoid or minimize problems that are encountered during the course of construction -problems that may arise due to ill assumptions, unanticipated conditions on site, public regulations, concerns with environmental laws and employee safety in the work place- the Project Manager should have effective risk management techniques. Some clients have been requiring the contractors to agree upon sharing the liability in instances when possible losses are encountered due to these risks, this move is to encourage the Project Managers as well to take risk management very seriously since failing to do so with greatly hurt the progress of the project and put the client at a disadvantage.

The Project Manager's task is to consider in detail and subject to rigid analysis possible risks present in the project and then create a common concordance with the client as to how these risks are to be shared. The Project Manager should make these risks less harsh during construction by cautiously choosing the materials and equipment that would be used along with keenly supervising construction among these risks.

The average pay of a Project Management in a year is around $ 84,000 and their possibility for future success in the industry are looking very great with a projection of expected growth of around 17 per cent by this decade alone.

The People involved with the Construction Project

The Project Manager is not the only person who is highly involved in construction. In fact, a Project Manager may have the best ideas in the world but without manpower, his ideas will never see fruition. So who exactly are the participants in construction job?

- **The Owner** – If you're reading this book, chances are you are the *owner* of an upcoming construction project. The owner is an individual or group who provides the capital for the construction project. The entirety of the owner's investments may come from his/her own pool of resources or from an outside financing source. All these will be explained with further detail later on.

- **Prime Contractors** – Prime contractors are responsible for a majority of administrative responsibilities regarding the project. Their main responsibility is to make sure that the entirety of the contract will have no loose ends. There are also other roles a prime contractor must fulfill depending on the project. These roles will be discussed throughout this book.

- **Subcontractors** – Subcontractors are usually hired by prime contractors to handle smaller and more specific parts of the contract. Keep in mind that if you're planning to become your own construction manager, you will also help in soliciting bids from subcontractors.

- **Engineers** – Engineers are responsible for specific designs and systems as required by the construction project. They have varying responsibilities, from the structure to the utilities of the project. An engineer's role is more on the technical side whereas a construction/project manager is more in executing the project with the desired quality and within budget. More specifically, an engineer can help you if your construction project has unusual site conditions or contains unconventional designs. In which cases, you may be required to have your building plans stamped and approved by a qualified engineer.

Additional Manpower for a Construction Project:

- *Plumbers*

- *Interior Designers*

- *Carpenters*

- *Machine Operators*

- *Foremen*

- *Architects*

- *Electricians*

Pros and Cons of Hiring a Prime/General Contractor

There are known benefits and disadvantages of hiring a general contractor for your construction project. Take note that the pros and cons in the following list apply *only if* you do not hire an architect:

Pros:

**Hiring a General Contractor is the easiest and simplest method to complete a medium-large sized construction project because the team are accustomed to working with each other and will be

motivated to finish each area of work so that their colleagues are not held up.

**A competent General Contractor will most likely have a list of competent subcontractors. The only disadvantage with this is that you need to know who is accountable, i.e. the General Contractor or the subcontractor, in the case of default.

**A General Contractor will shoulder all the administrative responsibilities involved with the construction project. This is a great use of good resources because they will have great experience in being able to cost jobs and get them done to a set schedule.

Cons:

**Hiring a General Contractor requires a great deal of trust from the owner's side but if the company is highly established and has a wonderful reputation, why not?

**The shortcomings of a General Contractor will have a negative effect on the rest of your team's output. This is important to consider, especially when you have different areas of work that need to be performed in conjunction with each other.

**Your influence in negotiations is slightly limited because the general contractor will assume responsibility over his workers instead of seeing you as the main boss on the site. It needs to be made clear that the project manager's word is final so that the general contractor is under no illusion about his part in the job.

Tip: Refer to Chapter 6 for a complete guide on how to choose a contractor.

Depending on the type of residential structure to be built, additional manpower with specific skill sets may be required. Note that there will be slightly different rules for assembling a construction team for *self-managed* projects. Still, most of them are composed of the people above. In Chapter 6, their functions will be further explained to help you in finding the appropriate person for each position.

Specialist workers are people that are always in demand. If you do need steel workers or workers that do tasks a little out of the ordinary, you will need to allow for them to have plenty of notice because these are workers who will be needed on other jobs. Installing steel joists, for example, may be needed where old walls are being taken down to provide a house with an open plan concept. The same applies to those who work with under floor heating because the new systems, which are earth friendly, are popular and take time to install. Only use those contractors that know their job well because inexperienced contractors in this field can produce alarming results.

Now that we've gone through the nature of a residential construction job, let's discuss The Construction Project Management Life Cycle in the next chapter. Remember that whether you are working for individuals or for a company, the expectations are very similar. Perhaps you are given more scope working for a company because you won't have potential owners trying to change your plans. However, it's your job to see to it that plans are not changed and that your workforce is kept on track at all times during the contract. The following chapters will give you a good overview of what it takes to be a Construction Project Manager and will also show you the reasons why or why not you should consider this position. There are pros and cons and once you see the full picture, you will be able to make up your mind for yourself, depending on your own strengths and weaknesses.

Chapter 3: The Initiation Phase

Chapter Objectives:

**The Importance of Finalizing an Idea before Starting a Construction Project*

**Basic Risk Management and Evaluation*

**Outline for Estimating Costs*

As all other projects are, construction management starts with an idea, which directly comes from what you wanted to build. Would that be a house, a building, a railway system, a park, or anything that allows development to occur? But when you have an idea, you need to have it evaluated in reference to verifiable scales so that its merits will be accurately determined. What you need to remember is that until an idea is viable, only then can project management commence.

The initiation phase is the phase of project management where the project is slowly setting out, the idea for the construction design is further being dug into and explained, detailed, clarified and developed until a full concept has been born out of a simple idea. The primary objective of this phase of construction management is to be able to assess the project's quality of being doable. In this stage the players are slowly being casted, where assignment of roles such as who is in charge of undertaking and materializing the concept, and who the primary characters involved are, these details are being finalized.

An idea can come from two sources: internal and external. Internal ideas come from within an organization or an individual. An example would be when a homeowner thinks about turning an empty lot into an investment by deciding to create an apartment complex there. External ideas come from outside sources. An example would be when a real estate developer or a construction company approaches a landowner and offers a proposal to build a residential complex in the homeowner's land.

When it comes to evaluating the viability of an idea, there are standard steps that need to be undertaken. These steps depend on the source of the idea. Nonetheless, whether or not you're an individual representing a construction company or you're working on your own, these steps you'll find below will help you analyze and evaluate the potential rewards offered by an idea.

The steps involved for internal projects pose a considerable degree of risk because it is something that you're planning to do on your own. If you're undertaking a project in behalf of a construction company, the amount or risk you need to prepare for is higher. Here are the steps you can follow:

- Conducting market research
- Creating a summary of proposed tasks
- Estimating costs
- Listing stakeholders
- Analyzing risks and rewards
- Scoping

Under market research, the steps involve the following components:

- Building a plan and specifying features
- Identifying potential locations (only if applicable)
- Analyzing financial needs
- Projecting sales price (if the property is intended to be sold or to generate revenues)

In contrast to construction projects that are initiated internally, external projects have lower amounts of risks. This is because someone outside initiated the project, which entails a degree of preparation. It would be safe to say that even before someone comes to you offering a proposal, preliminary steps would have been undertaken in order to obtain a buy in from you. Once you get a proposal, go through the evaluation process through these steps:

- Creating a summary of proposed tasks

- Estimating costs

- Listing stakeholders

- Analyzing risks and rewards

- Stating the scope of the project

Now, when does a construction or a project manager come in? First, it would be safest for you to invite a project manager across all situations involving property construction. Note that while building a house looks far less demanding than when building a commercial structure, realize that project managers are essential in ensuring that the goals of a construction process are achieved as well as making sure that construction progresses according to stakeholder specifications.

Second, if you were an individual representing a construction company, it would be best to bring in a project manager. Note that in some cases, the project manager can also be the same individual representing a company in which case, the problem about who to bring in is eliminated. And finally, if you are a homeowner looking forward to build a residential structure, you'll need all the help you can get from a project manager so you can focus your time in supervising the construction.

It is in this initial phase that the project leader accomplishes a written proposal which contains all the details regarding the conceptualized idea, from the feasibility of the project to the persons involved. Project proposals often come in forms of business plans where the summary of how the owners, managers and/ or other stakeholders intend to organize the project and implement its construction and completion. The potential sponsors involved in the project will then appraise the proposal and in the event that the proposal is approved, they will then jumpstart the construction project by providing the required budget. The approval of the project sponsors signals when the project has formally started.

Once a project manager comes in, you automatically become the stakeholder of the project. As a stakeholder, you'll work closely with the project manager until the project is completed. For now, these are the steps you need to be involved in:

- Creating the project proposal

- Reviewing the project proposal

- Approving the project proposal

- Transitioning the project to the planning phase

Once the steps above are completed and that you do not have any more concerns, you're ready to move on to the planning phase. That means in plain English that you need to have drawings of the proposed building that the owner agrees upon and that the authorities will eventually pass through their planning department. Bear in mind that objections may be raised if you are placing a home in an area of conservation or if there are homes that are adversely affected by what you propose to do. If you are cutting the light from an adjoining property, expect objections.

Thus, the property that you are building should be acceptable to its environment. If it is not, then the likelihood of planning approval will lessen. You need to discuss all of this whether the plan is an internal one or an external one and your plans need to incorporate all of the elements required by clients but also take into account what is acceptable code within the area in question. All safety requirements will have to be taken into account which is why architectural drawings need to be to scale and need to show where sufficient support is provided, what materials are going to be used and how this fits into the environment in which you propose to place it.

If the home is residential but the area is industrial, you need to have good reasoning so that you can take up the matter with local authorities and get the planning approval that you need to commence the project. Expect to have inspections because at different levels of the work, experts who work for the authorities normally carry these out. It will be your job to liaise with them and to give them as much information as you can.

Being a project manager means working before the first trowel is lifted, to get the plans approved and the measurements correctly represented by the architect which also represent what the client requires.

Estimating Possible Costs

Not everyone has the money to splurge on home renovation/construction. Homeowners are almost always limited in their budget – which is why it's crucial that you first estimate possible costs related to the construction. A rule of thumb with residential construction is that you should not fix a budget until the preliminary engineering process is over. This particular stage will help you establish a baseline for future construction costs. Keep in mind that the estimation process is consistently updated to reflect what has been done and the new information that comes in for the project. Studies reveal that establishing a baseline too soon actually results to higher construction costs that you would want to avoid.

The cost estimate in every construction project management plan should always conform to exactly, or almost exactly the precise amount of expenditures that need to be financed. Transparency is also one requirement that needs to be considered when finalizing cost estimates. This characteristic is often what investors or sponsors are trusting on, that they know just precisely where their money has been allocated. And finally, the breakdown of the cost estimate should be as reliable as possible. You would not want to time and again present another set of proposal with realigned or revised cost estimates just because you were not able to project the exact required amount from the start. This move will most definitely put off your sponsors.

The criticality of the cost estimates is especially of importance for small project ventures, such as simple residential projects, because of the restricted financial resources. The use of standardized practical methods created to function for cost estimation will enable project leaders and/ or project managers to have a better picture of the computation for cost estimate. These methods can provide project leaders enough reliability and accuracy as is required of cost estimates. And having dependable cost estimates would greatly contribute to the success of the project construction.

Refer to Chapter 6 – Assembling your Construction Team for a list of people who can help you with estimates. Additionally, you can skip ahead to Chapter 7 – Guide to Bidding for the applications.

Here's a step by step breakdown on how to approach estimating:

Understand the plan, making sure that there is a well-created blueprint for the construction. It's important to note that the blueprint must be exact with defined measurements and placement for estimation. Many homeowners are of the belief that a rough sketch would be enough for Project Managers to go on but this is not the case. Push for a concrete blueprint that offers accurate information for a near accurate estimate.

Create a list of every job, activity or product that needs to be done or ordered. It's usually a good idea to create a list in chronological order. For example, put down an estimate of the land acquisition followed by ownership transfer expense, cost of having a plan drawn up, price of feasibility studies made on the residential area (if any), cost of construction materials, labor, and insurance. Being specific is crucial in this case with NO expense left unlisted. A good Project Manager understands that there is no such thing as an immaterial expense.

Keep in mind that the list of expenses may vary depending on the inclusions in the residential construction. Make sure to check your own work multiple times for accuracy.

Have a second party double check your list to make sure that nothing is left out. Unfortunately, a lot of inexperienced Project Managers skip this part, causing problems in the long run.

Currently, Project Managers have several ways of arriving at an estimated cost. Depending on your personal preferences, the following are the different options available.

Resource Costing – This fairly known standard method for cost estimation requires the listing of all the resources you will need for the construction duration and then to add together each cost. Common resources utilized for construction are personnel labor and services, equipment, tools, raw materials and other possible professional fees. It is easy to acquire the latest quote for prices of materials, tools, and equipment from suppliers. It is wiser to purchase these items at larger and wholesale quantities because you get to save more out of these purchases. Estimating costs for personnel/ employees can easily be obtained by inquiring other projects which have the most similar objectives as the project you are undertaking. Bidding can also be done for purchases of materials as well as payment for people hired to carry out the work involved.

Stick Estimating – this is an old school method of estimating construction costs but highly accurate. Basically, what you do is create a list of the different jobs, the length of time it takes to finish them, the sub-contractors you will likely hire, and finally attach a cost to each one. When you use this method, you will have had to liaise with the workforce and will need to have received fixed estimates of what each element of the work will cost. In a case like this, if you are an individual get several quotations and make sure that you are comparing like with like and that exactly the same work is being proposed by all who quote for it. That way, you can decide between the quotations that are the ones, which realistically fit your requirements. You need to know that the timeframe for the work is also possible because the cheapest workforce may not be the most available workforce and once you have the go ahead, you really do need them to be reliable and there on the job on time.

Unit Cost Estimating – with this approach, Project Managers focus on the assemblies or lines needed for the job. A cost is attached per assembly, therefore allowing the Project Manager to arrive at an estimate faster. The integral unit or assembly refers to the size of the specific and unique part of the project. This may refer to surface area measurements in construction or particular areas in the building for construction. Estimating by cost per unit is highly recommended for small or unsophisticated projects. To be able to arrive at the total cost of a specific component of a project, all you have to do is simply multiply the total size of your particular unit to the unit cost.

Unit costing is a form of **Parametric Estimate** in which factors for construction such as the size and location of a room are referred to as parameters. Parameters, or units, are factors that are able to be measured and are used as variables for setting up a mathematical statement that will give out estimates as results. The product estimate calculated after multiplying the parameters of a project to the values obtained for the cost for every unit is called the parametric estimates.

As for the accuracy of the estimate, Stick Estimating offers a more refined result. Many Project Managers are using this method however since it only takes 1 week at the most to arrive at a number while Stick Estimating can take more than that.

Construction Calculators – thanks to computers, there are currently software that offer quick estimation services. These calculators are usually available through the Internet and offer estimation on basic construction needs. If you're hoping to get in-depth estimation however, the programs for sale are your best option. Keep in mind that geographical concerns must be taken into account when using calculators. These will only provide you with estimates and getting prices from contractors is much more likely to give you an accurate picture in your specific geographical location.

Estimating Books – before the advent of calculators, Project Managers used Estimating Books to help them compute costs faster. Simply put, these estimating books contain all the jobs during construction and their approximate costs. Project Managers simply need to identify the job they need and copy the cost indicated. The problem with this is that costs may become inaccurate due to industry fluctuation.

Empirical Methods – This technique is highly practicable for use in standard projects that have been a common procedure in some businesses. The application of empirical methods requires the use of either a cost estimating paper-based system or a software that has saved information on past project details, complete with statistical data of all the other past projects. All you have to do when utilizing this technique for your cost estimation is to supplement the software or paper system with the distinct attributes of your new project, based on the list that has been created grounded on past projects, add information on details of your current project under construction, and then ask the program to give out the overall cost analysis for your project. Using empirical methods for these kinds of projects saves a high amount of time and provides the users with very accurate results for cost estimation.

Historical Costing – This is in a manner similar to the empirical methods technique, except that this does not involve the use of software or paper-based system for cost estimation. Instead, this method simply uses the information used by a project that has only been closed in the recent past. Everything you need can be obtained from documentation of projects conducted in the past which is very similar to you current project. In the event that the project you are cost estimating is something unique, you can still make use of previous works of your company to establish a calculation based on the similar aspects of the completed project to your current project. Files of similar projects conducted by another company or contractor may also be useful, as long as these companies permit you access to these documents. The advantage of the historical costing technique is that it makes it possible for project leaders to have a rough prediction of succeeding costs in construction.

Historical costing can also be likened to **Analogous Estimate** where the process of cost estimation is also based on estimates conducted for other projects. The principle behind this technique is the logic that similar projects should have just about the same cost more or less. This assumption on the costing could then be adjusted by the person conducting the estimate, whether he or she would choose to increase or decrease cost estimate would be entirely up to his or her judgment, as she or he sees fit for the project.

Using one or more of these construction estimating techniques is usually a good idea if you want to verify the results of your computation. Again, repeated estimation is important through every part of construction to ensure that you are still within the boundaries of the budget.

What if it goes over budget? Finance is a finite resource in most construction projects and an estimate helps make sure that everything is done without spending more than necessary. Through constant estimation, the Project Manager is in the position to change specific aspects of the estimate, perhaps switch contractors or replace materials to fit in with the budget. This aspect of the construction usually requires the input of the homeowners.

What you do need to have costs for is everything and I mean everything that goes into the building, with that contingency fund of 35 percent to take account of anything that goes amiss. This is a wise amount because you may just come in on target and save yourself that 35 percent for the fancy items at the end of the job that actually make the home special and sale-worthy, if this is your intention.

Contingency funds are monetary values that are added into the estimate to account for unidentified resources for emergency purchase, call it your budget security blanket if you please but put simply this contingency fund is allocated in the budget estimate to provide for undetermined costs but are projected to be encountered during the course of construction. The basis for these contingency funds is the lessons learned for past project experiences. Setting aside of contingency funds prevents mortifying situations in project management and provides security for both the client and the contractor.

I have done another chapter after this one specifically aimed at individuals who are renovating as this really is a whole new ballgame as you may uncover extra work during the actual process of doing the work – that was not estimated for and that you didn't know you would have to pay for.

Go through the whole chapter because it gives you a good overview of everything that you need to think about when purchasing a house to renovate and when costing up the work that needs to be done so that you can project manage effectively. Remember, as an individual, it's very hard to put all those costs together, but if you want to be an efficient Project Manager, you really do need to get your head around all the different elements from the word "go" so that you are able to keep the project on course and not have any bad surprises along the way.

Chapter 4: Individual Purchase and Management of a Project

Chapter objectives:

***To give you a realistic overview of renovating*

** *To show you your job as a project manager*

** *To demonstrate the importance of keeping on track.*

The problems that you are going to encounter here are that you are emotionally involved in the purchase. You may not be looking at it from an investment point of view. If the home is going to be for you, it's easy to look past the faults that the house has and have a very romantic picture of what you want the house to be like after the renovation has taken place. If you have seen bad quality renovations, you will know that these happen because the project manager is not conversant with the real way to do this kind of work. They don't program the work correctly. They work hit and miss as and when they can afford different elements and what the house looks like at the end is a mixture of styles with nothing actually looking finished.

- What you need to be looking at are the following considerations:
- What type of walls do you have and are they solid?
- What insulation is being used in the house?
- What is the state of the roof?
- How recent are the electrics and would they pass code today?
- What sanitary items will you need to replace?
- What kitchen units will need replacement?
- The condition of the floors?

- The amount of available space within the home – does it need walls knocking down?

- Are these load bearing walls?

- What flooring will you use?

- What tiling will be used?

- Will you be changing doors and windows to bring them up to code?

- What heating is available?

- How much will it cost to replace electrics, plumbing and potential drainage?

You can see that the list of things is endless and there will be even more in the area where you live dependent upon the codes employed by the local authority. You also need to know what restrictions there are as far as exterior work goes and whether you are in fact permitted to change windows and doors – and this is something worthwhile finding out before you invest your money.

It's very good if you are permitted free reign on what happens within the house, but you also need to know a lot more than that. Can you have local contractors who can work in order? There are three main things to consider when you are setting up stages of work. These include:

The preparation work

Tearing out old items such as baths, kitchens, walls etc. can be done by you or by a laborer, which will cost less than employing a tradesman. However, there are some things that you need to bear in mind. If you come across any infestation within walls, you will have to call out professionals to deal with it. This may be mold or it may be an infestation of cockroaches, wasps or pests or it may be as serious as having active woodworm or termites. This may cause delays in your work and it may also increase costs, hence having that 35% contingency fund. You may also find that you have asbestos in the home and this is something you should never tackle yourself. Professional removal of this will have to be done.

The above preparation works can save you a lot of money but never cut corners with important items such as asbestos because it really is dangerous. What you can do safely is remove kitchen cabinetry that you are going to replace or even supervise the owners in doing this, remove toilets, bathroom items and strip out all flooring that is going to be replaced. The prep stage needs your supervision because there will be wires in walls, plumbing is attached to water supply and you may need to be there and have experts on site when things look like they need it. A house owner may not recognize problems, but you need to know to look out for all of the problems mentioned above while stripping the home back ready for renovation. Dampness is easier to tackle when you can actually see it, and while the house is stripped down, you may find that remedial works can be done at a lot cheaper than if you leave them and try to tackle them later.

First Fix

This is the period when work goes on behind the scenes. Plumbing pipes may need laying, heating ducts etc. may need to be cleaned and prepared for a new central heating system, you may need to have the house rewired. All of the work that goes behind walls falls under first fix, because this is when you will be punching a lot of holes in the walls and making a mess. Thus, it's wise to get all of this quoted for and out of the way before you can actually get on with the task of the more enjoyable part of decorating or renovating. If you are taking out any supporting walls or if the ceiling span is going to be too wide after you have taken down walls, you may also have to arrange for the installation of beams to support your ceiling structure. Insulation can also be done at this stage, but bear in mind that it can't be done until all electrical and plumbing work is finished as one may hamper the other.

Second Fix

This is when your plumber can put in showers or baths, toilets and sinks. The electrician can put all the socket covers on all over the house and leave it ready for decorating. Second fix also includes things such as installing heating appliances. At this stage, if you are considering having solar panels, this will be the time when the whole system is hooked up to work. Similarly with under floor heating, this will be the time when the whole installation comes together. So far you may only have seem the workings and the pipes under the floor. Second fix puts them all together and tests them.

Preparation for decoration

At this stage, you will be expected to inspect the whole property for anything that shows as a defect. The cracks in a ceiling, the missing baseboard, the finishes to the fixing of new windows and doors. Everything that needs to be finished and ready for painting should be done at this stage. Now is the time that all kitchen units can be finalized and your bathrooms and toilets should be ready for tiles to be installed. If you are putting down tiled floors, then the floor surface should be ready for it. That means on second floors that a screed will need to be laid or that a plywood finish will need to be used, so that there is no movement at all when the floors are walked on. Tiling must be finished and grouted before you are able to do the decoration. Preparation of all walls should be done and you should be satisfied that all wooden surfaces have been filled and rubbed down.

Decoration stage

At this stage of the work, there should be nothing structural to do. Yes, your client may decide that a change of fireplace hearth would make the place look nice, but this is something that is surface mounted and can be done at that stage. However, if you are taking on project management of your own work, you need to know that you can't keep chopping and changing your requirements because the tradesmen or contractors are liable to put the prices up and get very irritable about the changes because they also mean inconvenience. I remember one job where the electrician had finished all the wiring and the client suddenly realized that they wanted the lights to be obscured in the ceiling and they wanted a load of extra sockets that were not taken account of by the electrician at stage 1 and were therefore an inconvenience and caused a delay to the job.

The schematics need to be fully agreed before any of these stages is carried out so that everyone knows where they stand. It's vital to work like this because the order of the work is common sense. Although it may not be you who is doing the work, but instead you are project managing, someone will have to change things at a later time if the schematics are not thoroughly checked over at the time the work is actually implemented. That's bad management and as a project manager, you need to foresee the needs of the client and make the appropriate suggestions before the work gets to this stage.

The blueprints of the renovation are vital from the very beginning and these should mark all the changes so that all tradesmen are aware of what they need to do and your program or works makes allowance for the correct timing so that one contractor after another can work without getting in the way of another. It is not ideal to have plumbing and electrical contractors fighting for space to work simply because you haven't programmed the works in the correct manner.

Something to bear in mind on costs

When a house is bought by an individual, there may be financing involved. It this is the case, then any delay in the process of the work costs money. Remember that if you are buying the home to develop and sell on, then every day that goes over your schedule costs you more money. You will have utilities to pay for. You will have the cost of your loan (if any) and will not be completely free of extra expenses until the house is sold and shifted. Thus, be very aware of this and do not get complacent about your contractors turning up late for a job.

You need to have them tied down to a set date and time and know how much time they need to do the work, so that other contractors can be programmed into the schedule without losing valuable time. It's a very difficult thing to do, especially if you come across things that are not foreseen and need experts in to sort them out. Thus, make sure, as a project manager, that you know all the experts in your area that deal with bugs, dampness, mold and asbestos removal and that you are able to contact these people quickly and get them to respond in a timely manner. Did I tell you the project manager is also the one to provide adequate cups of tea and coffee to keep the workforce happy? In an individual project, you may find that your role is diverse, but that you need to be there and need to motivate your workers so that they reach their deadlines and are able to hand the home over to you on the programmed completion date. You also need to work within your set budget and keep an eye on any escalating costs.

A project manager that can keep track of all of the different elements of renovation and get permits sorted and inspections done will actually save money. That's why companies employ them and it's why their role is important. The project manager will have charts that show when work should be completed by and will be on the job to ensure that all the deadlines are met.

The project manager will spend a lot of time dealing with suppliers and will need to negotiate good prices for all of the items which are bought for a house and by letting suppliers know that you are in project management for the foreseeable future, you may be able to obtain great discounts on the items that you buy for the house. If not, try another supplier because your work depends on it. The kind of suppliers I am talking about are those that supply:

- Bathroom and sanitary equipment

- Windows and doors to current code

- Insulation suppliers

- Suppliers of white goods for kitchens and mud rooms

- Kitchen unit suppliers

- Heating installations

Wherever possible try to avoid having bespoke items since these are individually made and cost a fortune compared with off the shelf items. In one renovation, the cost of a new front door was so excessive that we decided to go for a standard door and make a fill in window down the side because it made the whole job much more cost effective and looked every bit as good. Watch out as you get to the stage of finishing because the shops can be very tempting and finishing off items such as faucets, shower heads, kitchen taps and all the trimmings can actually cost an awful lot of money if you don't keep your wits about you and keep the budget in mind at all times. If you really want those fancy taps, you will have to compromise in another area and it's your job as project manager to decide where you are prepared to compromise.

Chapter 5: Self-Managing a Project

Chapter Objectives:

**How to Prepare for Self-Managing a Construction Project*

**The Pros and Cons of Being your Own Construction Manager*

**Introduction to the Building Code of the United States*

After everything you've learned about project managers in Chapter 1, do you think you are fit to do the job yourself? Nothing about managing a construction project is easy or simple. While experience is a good requirement for guaranteed success, it doesn't mean you cannot handle a project yourself without it.

It well may be that the entire concept of project management can seem very intimidating to some, especially for those who have just recently heard and read of the concept and those who have little or no background at all when it comes to construction. For those who have had previous encounters with this concept, you have probably thought of elaborate projects such as the new World Trade Center or the Tokyo Tower. However, after reading through the previous chapters you may have already grasped the idea that construction project management can also be applicable to small scale business projects equally in the same manner it applies to large scale projects.

These small scale projects, even the simplest kind of residential renovations, can make use of efficient construction project management. All it takes for basic learners in the field is to take the risk of starting with the project.

Additionally, every successful construction/project manager had to start somewhere. Although there is no way for you to acquire extensive construction experience through reading the previous chapters alone, you can apply what you've learned and *acquire* those experiences through self-management.

Tip: Throughout the rest of this book, you can freely review the previous chapters as reference.

The Pros and Cons of being your own Construction Manager (CM)

Professional project managers are readily available to help you out in your construction. These project managers can greatly reduce the burdens and stress you may most probably encounter when planning to self-build. Hiring someone else to overlook the construction process from start to finish is a sensible choice for two reasons. One, you as the owner may not be confident with your own construction experience. If you manage to read and learn through this entire book, this particular reason should be eliminated. Two, you may be unable to invest all of your time overseeing the project due to certain circumstances.

Although in the selection of construction project managers or general builders the best does not all the time guarantee the cheapest ones, what is important in the selection of builders for your project is to find the one who can be affordable but at the same time able enough to finish with a good quality output. Another advantage of hiring professionals in construction projects is that these individuals often already have the right contacts to obtaining the best materials and supplies at the most sensible price.

Remember with me all the roles and responsibilities of a professional construction project manager we have laid out in the previous chapters. So in essence, once you hire a project manager, you also acquire for yourself the added benefits of all the things the project manager handles for you (given you selected a capable professional). You hire for yourself the skills necessary in order to have a clearly planned out and defined construction procedure within the constraints of your laid out budget and resources allotted for the project and all the output delivered within your agreed upon time frame.

Hiring an efficient construction Project Manager is equivalent to saying that you have allocated your resources to the promise that this individual will be able to provide better skillfulness to your construction site. This is not exactly a waste of good money. The Project Manager will be able to provide for you (in exchange for your payments of his or her professional fees) resources bought at the best deals, hassle-free transactions during the implementation of the project without the stresses that accompany construction delays, assurance that your building will be successfully finished on or before your set deadline within your allocated budget and with the least possible excessive worries.

On the other hand, people choose to self-manage construction projects. There have been success stories coming from people who have dived into self-managed construction projects head on and have emerged from the ordeal with a successfully accomplished output. From another point of view, there have been others who have seen and experienced how self-managing construction projects have consumed up most of their time, effort and resources.

Of course, deciding to be your own construction manager has its downsides. For one, it requires you to spend a great deal of your time throughout the project. A successful construction project from self-management requires your utmost commitment. Being your own construction manager will definitely limit your time for work, business, and family.

Despite these discouragements, a surprising many individuals have chosen to self-manage their construction projects for the following reasons:

1. **Saving Money** – Evidently, a lot of people choose to be their own construction/project managers with the thought of saving

money from hiring. The fees these professional construction project managers require are often times not a very budget friendly value. While this may be true for the most part, remember that *mistakes* in construction are also expensive.

2. **More Control** – A lot of people, especially owners, find it more desirable to self-manage a construction project. This is because they feel more 'in control' of the entire project. It is also true that self-managing an entire project is very satisfying.

3. **Exactly What You Want** – By being involved in all the phases of construction, you will be able to provide your input whenever necessary. You will also be able to make adjustments and decisions to suit both your preferences and the circumstances.

4. **Experience** – Completing a project will grant you relevant construction experience to prepare yourself for future project. Self-managing your first project may even open up an entirely new career path for you.

The decision to become your very own project and/ or construction manager means that you have recognized and accepted full well that you are taking complete responsibility for all your actions and every consequence that comes along your choices. In simpler terms, this means that if all goes well then you deserve all the bragging rights and confidence boost your project provides you, however, this may also mean that if anything goes wrong then you only have yourself to blame for wasted resources, time and energy.

As your own construction manager, you must always keep in mind that you need to organize the necessary inspections, supervise quality control, and coordinate with subcontractors and suppliers. You also need to establish an open communication between everyone involved throughout the project.

Also remember that as the construction manager, it is your job to make sure the project fulfills the different specifications of the *building code*.

The Building Code

The United States follows a model building code created and enforced for the protection of public health. These set of rules take into consideration the quality/type of approved materials, the structural soundness of the project, the location of the project, and other aspects including electrical systems, water systems, and so on.

Remember that even self-managed construction projects should comply with the existing building code.

In the US, there are two main codes: the *International Commercial Code* (ICC) and the *International Residential Code* (IRC). As of today, self-managing a construction project is applicable for residential constructions and renovations for the most part. On the other hand, a professional project manager is recommended for commercial buildings. When employing any staff to work on the job that you are supervising, you need to know that they are competent and can provide you with certification for important elements of the build such as electrical, gas and plumbing installations. You need these to be able to prove that the home is up to current code and the professionals that you hire should be competent to produce these.

Deciding what you can do yourself

Do you plan to be your own contractor/construction manager? Never forget the key principles of the construction management life cycle, from the initiation phase to the closing phase – which of those responsibilities can you fulfill with confidence? Another rule for success in construction: Unless you can guarantee a job well done, find someone else to do it! It's also a very hard job. Many people have been overwhelmed by being their own construction manager because of the diversity of the job. You need to check that all the blueprints are being adhered to, whether the permits you require are available, whether the day to day work is being done and also to chase up late suppliers, which, in the building trade, is something that is inevitable.

Where non-professional people take on construction management, often they don't have any idea how to do the job that they are expected to do by their client or by the contractors who work for them. Inexperience really will show and if you are taking on a task like this you need to show confidence and be able to make snap decisions, which won't delay the work being done.

Two Secrets for Success in Construction Management

In simpler terms, to have a successful construction project, a construction or project manager should focus on *planning* and *communication. Communication is of paramount importance. You need to be strong enough to get suppliers moving when delays happen. You need to be friendly enough to explain to workers any changes needed in their scheduled work.*

It's all on how well the layout is planned and how effective the plan is communicated throughout the entire team. Keep in mind that people in the construction industry are highly visual. They tend to communicate better with precise and detailed *illustrations*. Unless a construction plan is presented in this form, your construction team will definitely have trouble building it – if they even know what you want built!

Truth be told, *designing* is the most important aspect of the entire construction project. This is not a process to be rushed. Also make sure to produce absolutely complete and polished design specs. Commencing a construction project with just rough sketches will only bring you cost increases, conflicts, and much unwanted delays.

With a thoroughly completed construction plan, you can:

Clearly establish the quality standards you are expecting from your team

By the time that you have sorted out which workmen you will use, you will need to befriend them and talk about the quality of work that you expect. Talk to them and show them examples of the kind of work you want. Don't put up with defective work practices and make it clear from the beginning that you expect the work to be aesthetically pleasing and of the highest quality possible for the price.

Prevent cost overruns, disputes, delays, and disruptive change orders

This is probably one of the hardest tasks of the lot. The kitchen cabinetry arrives and the company has it wrong. Your measurements are not the same as theirs. You have to be able to overcome problems such as this and delays that it may cause. You may have disputes and misunderstandings with your contractors who may have interpreted something that you have asked them to do incorrectly. Perhaps the blueprint wasn't clear and all of these things zap your energy and you can't afford to let them slip. As construction project manager, it's your job to smooth the way, to find solutions and to please everyone and sometimes that's going to be hard. Cost overruns are difficult to deal with and if you keep everyone on budget and there are extra costs, these need to keep within the parameter of your contingency money so constant recalculation is vital to finishing the job on budget.

Acquire reasonable estimates from a number of different contractors (better accuracy)

Be careful to read these thoroughly as someone who looks cheaper at the outset may actually be more expensive because their quotation does not include the same elements as the more expensive ones. You need to be specific when you are ordering quotations in that every item on your list must be quoted for so that each quotation or estimate is actually pricing up the same things and can be compared in a like to like manner.

Present your project for getting a construction loan

Your construction/renovation plans are dependent on the *owner*, the *professional designer*, the *building contractor*, and the *stock plan book*. Of course, your construction plan may be the result of the collaborative effort of many. You may absorb ideas from sketches, magazine photos, or even science fiction movies. As long as you observe the building code (to be discussed in the next chapter), you're free to consider the most imaginative ideas you can concoct.

When you put together a construction plan, you need to know the current value of the property and have an idea of what the property will be worth once you have done to remedial work. The bank wants to know that there is a good chance that they will get a return should the loans be unpaid, but you also need to know the parameters within which you will work your budget. For example, if a house is worth $100,000 currently and your work will take that value to $150,000, will the work cost you more than $50,000? The reason why this is so important is that your client will want to know that the work you are performing on their house is worth it and that it's a solid investment.

Your management of the project should take into account all of the aspects mentioned above but it needs to go further than that. If a client cannot see a good return on their investment, they are likely to be upset by it. Therefore, having contacts in the real estate market may be a good idea so that you can reassure clients of potential values of a house once the work has been performed.

In the following chapters, we go over all the elements that are involved with the construction management role so that you can get a fuller picture before deciding to take this route. It can be a very profitable business venture, but unless you go in with your eyes fully opened to the possibilities and the potential hazards, it may not be the best investment of your time. You need to be prepared in advance for what the work involves and once you are, you are much better able to see whether this falls within your capability.

On "Grand Designs" which is a TV show broadcasted all over the world, project managers were usually homeowners who decided to take the bull by the horns and property manage themselves, rather than pay someone to do it for them. Many of them regretted the decision – not because they did a bad job – but because of the effect on their relationships and the amount of strain it put them to. Thus, you need to have an honest opinion of what this task entails before you start. If you are one who gets easily worried, it won't be the perfect job for you. There are so many variables and situations can change from day to day. Thus, this kind of work is more suited to someone who is flexible in their approach, calm in their demeanor and able to take good days with bad ones.

Chapter 6: The International Residential Code

Chapter Objectives:

**Basic Details You Need to Know about the International Residential Code

**The Crucial Requirements of the IRC for most Construction Projects

Another disadvantage of being your own construction manager is that you have a lengthy list of structural requirements to be aware of. Make sure you coordinate well with whoever is in charge of your design – be it an architect, an engineer, or your spouse. Furthermore, you need to oversee the entire execution phase to make sure these requirements are being duly fulfilled.

Basic Details You Need to Know about the International Residential Code

The International Residential Code (IRC) is a complete and independent residential code formulated by the International Code Council (ICC). This international standard sets minimum requirements and maximum limits for designing and constructing residential structures that shelters one- and two-family housing. This code is regularly updated, every three years, and evaluated comprehensively to cater to modern and novel materials and designs used for building constructions.

The fundamental reason or logic behind the restrictions included in the International Residential Code are all rooted with the intent of promoting public health, overall welfare and safety.

The International Residential Code is not as restrictive that it still renders enough flexibility for construction designers, managers and builders in their building procedures. These codes were simply created with the determined purpose of making sure residential buildings meet standards that will ensure the public's safety in the comforts of their homes.

The International Residential Code is very straight forward and will pose no difficulty whatsoever to construction workers and managers. In fact it requires little or no effort at all for owners and contractors to understand and implement these codes.

What is stated in the International Residential Code is a set of rules, principles and laws that cover all the basic aspects of building construction, namely, energy conservation, mechanical aspect, plumbing concerns, building details, electrical and fuel gas provisions.

The Crucial Requirements of the IRC for most Construction Projects

The IRC supplies the required specifications for residential construction projects including, but not limited to, *minimum room areas, sanitation, ceiling height, light, ventilation, heating, accessibility, restroom spaces, fire-resistant designs, flood-resistant structures,* and *means of egress.* Here is a brief overview of the most important specifications of the IRC:

- **Minimum Room Area** – Any residential structure is required to have at least one habitable room. This room must have a floor area of at least *120 square feet.* Additional rooms must have a floor area of at least 70 square feet with the exception of kitchens. In case of sloping/dome ceilings, the measurement for the habitable floor area may be reduced to the areas where the ceiling reaches less than 5 feet from the floor (less than 7 feet for furred ceilings).

- **Minimum Ceiling Height** – Habitable areas within the structure should have a distance of at least 7 feet from the ceiling to the floor. These areas include restrooms, bathrooms, laundry rooms, hallways, bedrooms, and basements.

  o There should be no portion of the area wherein the distance between the ceiling and the floor is less than 5 feet; otherwise that particular section will be deemed "inhabitable".

  o Certain fixtures in bathrooms, such as showers or tubs equipped with showerheads, should have a ceiling height of at least 6 feet and 8 inches (given that these fixtures can be used for their intended functions).

  o In the basement, inhabitable areas must have a ceiling height of at least 6 feet and 8 inches. This limit does not apply for beams, ducts, or girders. In which case, the minimum ceiling height is reduced to 6 feet and 4 inches.

The problems that you may encounter here are when you are doing up an old house that didn't apply these codes or when you are putting in a ceiling that is lower to make a room look more modern. If you need to put in beams for extra support, these need to conform to the ceiling height restrictions shown in local code. Another area where you may find that there are restrictions is where you have existing steps that don't conform. Adjustment may have to be made so that they do conform and this can involve extra costs.

- **Light and Ventilation Specifications–** All habitable areas must have a sufficient amount of natural ventilation through doors, windows, louvers, or other passages that allow outdoor air.

  o Additionally, these ventilation systems must be easily accessible and usable by anyone within the structure.

  o The area of these ventilation systems must be at least 8% of the floor area for windows and 4% of the floor area for everything else.

  o Glazed areas are no longer required for rooms with access to artificial illumination with at least 65-lux capacity.

  o For bathrooms, a minimum of 3 square feet is required for glazing. ½ of this minimum requirement should be openable. This is no longer required if using an approved artificial light source and exhaust system.

  o Natural ventilation through the use of a sunroof or patio covers is allowed *only* if more than 40% of the sunroom walls are open / enclosed with *fly screens*.

  o Exterior stairways, including the treads and landings, are required to have adequate illumination. For interior stairways, an artificial light source capable of at least 11 lux of illumination is required and must be situated at the center of the landings and treads. Additionally, this light source must be operable from both sides of the stairway. Lastly, exterior stairways leading to the basement must have a light source at the bottom landing.

  o Every pane of glazing material used must come with the manufacturer's designation. This must specify the type of glass, who applied the designation, and the applicable safe glazing standards.

o Any glazing material must be installed in such a way that it couldn't be removed without being destroyed. It could be sandblasted, ceramic-fired, acid/laser etched, or embossed.

o The edges of glazing material must be *smooth* all throughout. The compatible glazing material used for louvered windows and jalousies must have the prescribed thickness of at least 3/16 inches or 5 millimeters.

As you can see, this is rather a lot of information to retain, but you can refer to this book if in doubt and check that everything conforms to standards, which are preset by the IRC for the specific purpose of safety. You can't get around these codes. They must be adhered to and it's your job as construction overseer that they are upheld.

· **Heating Specifications** – All habitable rooms in the structure must have a heating system with the capability to maintain at least 68°F *for* winter design temperatures less than 60°F.

· **Sanitation Facilities** – The IRC also requires a lavatory, a water closet, and a shower/bathtub for all dwellings. Additionally, residential structures should have at least one kitchen area with a sink. Plumbing systems must also be able to receive from the approved water supply and must be connected to an approved sewage system.

· **Bathroom/Restroom Clearance Spaces** – Toilet and bathroom facilities must have the required clearance specifications to not impede their uses.

o Toilets are required to have at least 21 inches usable space *in front*.

o Sinks are required to have at least 21 inches usable space *in front*.

- o Tubs must be adjacent to a wall and required to have at least 21 inches clearance on the *other side*.

- **Means of Egress** – Each residential structure should have at least one egress door.

  - o With the door opened by 90°, the clearance between the face of the door and the stop should be at least 32 inches. Also make sure that the egress door is side-hinged.

  - o The egress door(s) must be operable from the *inside* of the structure without special requirements such as keys, passcodes, and other locking devices.

  - o The egress door must have a clearance of at least 78 inches in height.

Other than the common specifications listed above, the IRC has several other articles regarding one to two family dwellings. Make sure you are aware of these specifications, especially when handling bigger and more complex/sophisticated construction projects. To be more specific, here are the additional articles that are included in the IRC:

**Fire-Resistant Construction

**Flood-Resistant Construction

**Storm Shelters

**Smoke Alarms

**Site Address

**Emergency Escape and Rescue Openings

**Garages and Carports

**Guards and Window Fall Protection

**Elevators and Platform Lifts

**Protection of Wood/Wood-Based Products against Decay

**Protection against Termites

**Foam Plastic

**Carbon Monoxide Alarms

If you think your project will be affected by the articles listed above, it's a must for you to review the building code prior the planning phase.

As a construction manager, you cannot afford to overlook a single aspect of the IRC. Make sure that your building plans are designed from the ground up to conform to these existing codes. An architect will be aware of these codes and should draw their blueprints using these codes. Make sure that you have confidence in the ability of your architect and ask what recourse you have if any of their drawings are not up to code. That's quite important because that means that they may have to supply alternative drawings if theirs do not meet all the specifications that are insisted upon by the IRC.

Your best bet in this regard is to check everything and make sure that the rules have been adhered to. It's no good finding out after the work has been done because this isn't cost effective and you will have to rip out what's been done and redo it so that current codes have been adhered to. That's neither economically viable nor good for relationships with contractors.

When employing contractors, it's a good idea to interview them and to find out what their experience and qualifications are before you get to the hiring stages. You can do this while you are gathering quotations for the work and getting to know your contractors is a really good way forward because they will be able to produce their qualifications and do the work to the specifications that you put forward.

If you are using new products that contractors are not accustomed to, this needs to be thoroughly discussed. In this day and age, this is quite possible as new forms of insulation and new forms of block work are available which are considered "green" as well as geothermic heating and the installation of solar panels. You really need to have people who are qualified to do this, rather than trust a general contractor to deal with products he knows nothing about.

You also need to know the R-values of all insulation because not all insulation is equal and if you live in an area, which suffers from either too much heat, or too much cold this is an aspect, which is going to affect the lifestyle of those who live within the house. Talk to dealers and find out the specifics so that you can offer your client the best value for the area in which they live, rather than the cheapest option, which may give disappointing results.

Chapter 7: The Planning Phase

Chapter Objectives:

**The Importance of the Planning Phase

**Creating your Construction Schedule

**The Important Parts of the Planning Phase

Once a construction project is approved, the natural tendency for those involved is to go to work right away. After all, executing a project comprises the bulk of the construction project life cycle. But while it is tempting to proceed with the hands-on aspect of the project right away, you can't afford to miss something integral to construction. This is why planning the project needs to come before execution.

Essentially, planning should answer three important questions:

- What must be done?
- How should it be done?
- Who does the job?

The planning phase typically involves the organizing and preparing of the task at hand in the construction project. This phase includes the act of improving and elaborating details in the project by specifying the activities that need to be done in order to attain the project aims, goals and targets. It is also in this phase that the monetary information in the project is broken down into more explicit details and with as much information for allocation as is possible.

It is also at this phase that detailed information on the number of people as well as the roles of individuals selected to be part of the project team is further expounded. The purchasing of materials, tools, equipment and all the other stuff required for a functional construction procedure starts in this phase of the project.

Also, the planning phase further develops and executes the project plan in more detail and of the utmost attention to even the simplest and minutest of concern. The primary goal that must be addressed during this phase of the construction project is to grasp an understanding of the how and in what way or manner or by what means the project will be carried out. Additional concerns include acquisition of all the necessary resources for a smoother operation and more efficient finishing of project goals. It is in this phase that most of the project designing, preparing and purchasing takes place but all these activities may still continue even towards the completion of the project. As long as the finishing touches for the project have not yet been done, the planning continues as a response to fresh challenges and circumstances presented while constructing the project. During the entire period of construction, project leaders and workers never stop planning activities for the project.

It is true that the project proposal contains vital information that allows a project to thrive; a plan is necessary in order to ensure that every task that falls under execution is properly carried out. Time, money, and effort are resources you cannot afford to waste.

The planning phase is essentially composed of the following items:

- The scope of the project
- The scope management plan
- Cost management
- Quality assurance
- Human resources
- Communication channels
- Construction schedule

- Contracting and contract administration

- Project baselines

The items above only represent a part of that which is considered under the planning stage, but fairly gives you an idea about the nature of the planning phase. In effect, the planning phase is a lot different from the initiation phase. It also serves as the foundation of the execution phase because until a project is completed, the things discussed under the planning phase will constantly be revisited. This makes the planning phase characteristically iterative. This means that you will never get away from what you've planned hence the need for a project plan.

To help you through the planning process, here are a few things you need to consider:

The order the work will be done

We have already discussed this in a previous chapter, but you need to work out the process for your particular house, to include Labor and clearing of the site, first fix, second fix and finishing of the property. Sorting out the order means booking the contractors and finding out their availability, it means setting up time scales and it also means being sure that the workers that you need are available to work in the order that you need them to. Remember that your clearance people should be the first ones in and that these don't have to be that specialized. It does, however, help to have people who are relatively strong and very willing to work on the areas you direct them to. It's worthwhile hiring a waste skip at this stage, so you can remove rubble and debris from the site, leaving the house clean for your contractors to get on with what they have to do.

The personnel needed to do the work

You have to decide what part of the work you will actually undertake, if any, and have plumbers, electricians, tilers, decorators, etc., all programmed in to do their work.

The worker's schedule

Part of your duty as the construction manager is to keep the flow of the work going and thus having a schedule which shows you clearly which staff should be on site at which time will show you immediately if someone has messed up the schedule. This schedule should also include what you expect each of the contractors to do on any given date.

Selection of the subcontractors (if applicable)

If you are making a selection of subcontractors based on the estimates provided, you need to make this pretty soon, so that you can book each of them into your schedule. If you delay, this may mean that they get onto another job and are no longer available within the time scale set by you.

Whether or not the subcontractors will provide their own materials

Usually electricians and plumbers like to supply their own materials because they are accustomed to working with materials of a certain quality that they are familiar with. They should have included this on their estimates so this should not include you in extra payments. However, if you are supplying anything such as tile adhesive for your tilers, you will need to make sure it's available as and when they need it. The same with tiles, worktops etc. you need to order these so that your workmen have them available as soon as they are needed.

Who will be responsible for the materials?

Let all contractors know that although you will ensure that the property is locked at night, they will need to be responsible for their own materials. It is commonplace that materials are stolen when a house is not lived in, so be sure to lock the home and keep all materials under lock and key, asking contractors to take the necessary precautions with looking after their own materials while fulfilling the contract.

The budget for each item involved in the construction

You need to keep up to date spreadsheets on the budget for each item that you will use in the house. If one costs less than anticipated, that gives you more contingency, but you need to keep an eye on costs and also take into account the additional cost of delivery to the site. This includes everything and it is a good idea to keep these costs separate from the labor costs of contractors, so that you know exactly where the budget is at any given time for the materials that will be used for the renovation.

The people who will inspect the work

When you apply for permissions, you are usually given comprehensive instructions about inspections. Don't ignore them. If you continue to build without thinking of the inspections, it could cost you extra money, because these inspections are designed to be done at different stages of the work being performed. Make sure that you have your dates of completion of whatever they need to inspect and that you make arrangements with them to call and inspect the work, which has been done, to see that it complies with code.

The types of work that needs to be inspected

When you put in for a permit, it is always made clear what needs to be inspected. This can include all kinds of aspects and depends upon where you are located geographically. Of particular interest in country environments, you may be asked to inspect any drainage system from the property to avoid pollution. Respect the requirements because you can't just fill in the septic tank without them inspecting it first. Read all your planning papers thoroughly and make yourself aware of what needs further inspection and the telephone numbers of appropriate officials who deal with these inspections.

Adjustment measures for sub-par work

As the Construction Manager, you have to deal with problems that arise from the work that is performed. It's not an easy task but you do need to watch out for sub-par work. If you need to ask someone to do something over again, then it should be at their cost, not yours, unless the instructions that were originally given were unclear. In that case, you may have to bargain with the contractor and try to get him to take half of the loss. A reasonable contractor will do that. If the work done by the contractor does not conform to your agreement or the plans drawn by the architect then that's his fault and the cost should be borne by him. In fact, you may encounter resistance, but you need to put yourself over as confident and try to win the contractor over in as nice a way as possible, if you want him to continue work for you.

The difficulty that you are going to have is when the work is sub-par and you don't think that the contractor is capable of doing better work. You may have to lay the contractor off in a case like this, which can hit your schedules until you are able to find another contractor. That's why it's so important to stress the quality you expect at the outset.

The person who pays and when the bills are paid

You should let your contractors know when bills will be paid. If you are working for a client, they will need to have funds available for these payments. Stage payments are quite usual but never let a client pay in full until fully satisfied that all the work has been done to the standard you require. Always keep a little retention back if there is remedial work that is needed.

The times when a client will be allowed to inspect the job site

You will be in control of this and sometimes clients can be very pushy. If you are creating a dream home for someone who is not accustomed to seeing a building site, it's best that you go over all the details and then ask them only to attend when you need to agree on materials for specific tasks, such as tiling, kitchen worktops etc. The problem with having the client on the premise all the time is that people are fickle. They see the different stages of the house renovation and come up with ideas to incorporate that may actually not be included in the budget. Make the budgetary factor very clear to them and also make it clear that once everything has been agreed, changes cannot be made at a later date without this costing more.

Adjustment measures in case the client changes his mind

I know that it is very irritating indeed, but clients have a habit of introducing new elements when you have already done work as agreed. People do this. They want a different colored worktop, or want you to incorporate an island when you have made no allowance for this in the budget or the work schedule. When this happens, you have to be fairly strong and ask them to have a certain amount of trust in what you are doing rather than second guess it and come up with new things. They also need to know that extras cost extra money and that it will be their budget that will be affected by it.

It's far better to get together with the client and give them alternatives at the beginning of the job. Having samples available is useful. Let them choose certain finishes, colors for the rooms, etc. and then when they do want to change their minds, try to talk them out of it on economic grounds. If you have to make adjustments, then they will have to pay for them and the inconvenience is sometimes very annoying.

The questions above are only a representation of the things that the people involved in construction needs to think about. Perhaps the greatest responsibility falls on the Project Manager who needs to do a lot of thinking about how to approach the construction project. Nonetheless, the result of the planning phase is a document called the project plan. The project plan ideally should have the following components:

Construction schedule

Scheduling works hand in hand with planning. Others may even consider Scheduling as a small part of the planning phase while others sees it as a distinct activity. The main purpose of scheduling is to arrange the timing of tasks to meet a deadline. Since most project constructions are limited by time, the scheduling process makes sure that the system is seamless and that everything started is finished within a dictated amount of time.

There are currently several methods being used for Scheduling in Project Management. The most common one is called Work Breakdown Structure (WBS), which involves an estimate of time spent on each job. A resource list is also included in the WBS, allowing the Project Manager to choose a possible resource if it becomes necessary.

The estimate is usually supplied by the resource or the people who will be doing the job. Project Managers chasing a specific completion date may seek out other providers to ensure that the construction adheres to the contract. A "What If" scenario should also be factored in together with a Critical Chain Method and Risk Multiplies.

The construction schedule is created by coming up with a Work Breakdown Structure (WBS) and a WBS dictionary. The dictionary identifies all aspects of the work to be done. The schedule being developed here is the same as what you might see in an office, but it also considers the following factors:

- Task sequencing so that each job follows a logical order
- Time estimates for a specific job to be completed
- Specification of the individuals who are responsible for each task
- Scheduling method controls so that the WBS is stay functional throughout the life of a project

Like Estimating and Planning, the Scheduling Phase must be constantly updated. Doing so will help Project Managers adjust their plan in accordance with the overall goal of the residential project. Ideally, the baseline value of the job must be the same as the

Estimation at Completion for the schedule to be considered healthy. Of course, this might not always be the case.

Cost control

The cost control plan addresses three needs:

- Cost estimate of each of the tasks needed to build the structure
- Budget statement of the entire project
- Statement of the method to be employed in monitoring project costs throughout the span of construction

Quality assurance

There are two primary parts under quality assurance:

- The quality of project management and the resulting structure
- The processes to be implemented in order to ensure quality maintenance throughout the project

If we go back to the example provided in Chapter 1, you'll see how quality plays an integral role in the construction business. In order to achieve the goals set for Clearpoint Residences, everyone involved in construction has to agree to quality standards. The same concept applies to every structure to be constructed. Whatever the client wants or the management wants, it can be achieved by adhering to the highest precepts of quality.

Human Resource

Human resource mainly deals with manpower. Since most construction projects are subcontracted, careful consideration should be taken when it comes to hiring, training, supervising, and even firing individuals who are part of the project. Understandably, these functions are delegated to the Project Manager who, from the onset of the project, is responsible in hiring people and managing them until the construction project is completed.

If, however, you deem a project manager unnecessary and choose to be your own construction manager, it is imperative for you to be knowledgeable with the key positions regarding a significant construction project. These positions will be explained with more detail in the *next chapter*.

Communication

There are two keywords under communication: accessibility and timeliness. The duration of a project does not determine the kind of communication mechanisms to be employed. What matters is that the stakeholders, the management, and the construction project team regularly get in touch with each other to discuss whatever it is that need to be taken care of. There are also times when a roadblock is encountered, thus the necessity of putting up communication alternatives and methods to keep things running. Again, it is the Project Manager's responsibility to make sure that everyone involved in construction can reach out to each other.

What you may not realize as a Construction Manager is that you act as the go between, between the client and the workforce. You act as a go-between between the suppliers and the workforce. Your communication skills are therefore very necessary to the smooth running of the project. Basically, you need to know how to deal with people and that's sometimes a very tricky task. It's important that you get to know your clients well and are able to communicate effectively with them. Don't let them rule you. They have trusted you to be in charge of the project and when things start to get difficult between you, it's time for a site meeting to decide on final things that make a difference to the work that you are doing. Similarly, you will have to use strong communication skills to chase up your suppliers and find out where things are that have not arrived on time. Be stern with suppliers because he who is the most put out, but calm, will be he who gets the attention of the suppliers and gets them moving.

Risk Management

While risks exist in almost everything we do, they are avoidable with proper planning. The risk management plan is divided into two sections that will help you avoid risks: identification and analysis of risks and the corresponding actions to take, and a plan of action to monitor the different stages of the project so that risks can be addresses before they damage the construction process. But again, risks are avoidable, but a plan is still needed in order to make sure that everyone moves in the same direction when circumstances are not good. You also need to ensure that all workmen who are employed at the house have their own insurances for the work that they are producing, so that the client is reassured at all times. If the roof leaks after installation, it's the roofer that must put this right. If there are electrical problems, then the electrician must bear the cost of putting that right and should always have adequate insurance to deal with any claims made by the homeowner.

Contract administration

This component also includes purchasing, and covers areas like contract management, subcontractor management, and purchase management. Note that the subcontractor management part need not be there when the project will not be subcontracted. A short chapter about contracts is found in the latter parts of this book. It is, however, your job as Construction Manager to oversee all areas and to make sure that the workforce are keeping their end of the bargain in producing work which is up to standard. You also need to chase suppliers when errors are made and also when items are arriving with you late and causing delays to the project. Remember, delays cost money.

Project baselines and documentation

Project documentation contains additional notes that accompany the project plan. Additions can be the project contact, details about the site survey, blueprints, permits, policies, warranties, and installation guidelines.

On the other hand, the project baseline serves as a point of comparison to determine whether or not a project is moving forward as desired with respect to deadlines and costs. Along the life of the project, when costs go beyond the identified baseline, it is safe to say that the prepared budget is not being followed. The same thing works with schedule. If the team does not complete a specific task in a given deadline, delays are expected to impact the overall progress of the project.

You need to remember that each day has the potential of causing you problems. Each day will be different and present different problems. People who work as construction managers or overseers say that they gain a great deal of expertise over the course of their work because they have to know the trades and what each is expected to do. If they didn't, they wouldn't be able to do the jobs that they do.

Although contracts are covered in a different place, I cannot emphasize enough how much you need to add a clause at the end of any contracts about work which is not finished on time and add a penalty clause which means that you will get the work at a reduced cost if the work is not completed on time. That's important incentive for your workers to get everything working in the right order and finished at the right times, ready for other contractors to start their work.

It's not all hunky dory in the project/construction manager field of work. In fact, it's very hard work indeed. You get to deal with clients who can't decide upon the color or size of a bath, which want to change the tiling after you've already done it and who can't decide upon colors for their main living areas. Add to that, they also want you to change things at a late stage of the game and you need to remember that although you may have done everything in accordance with their wishes, their wishes can change and often do, leaving you feeling unfulfilled and quite frustrated in the work that you have to do. The Property Brothers on the TV have a very professional way of dealing with this by locking the client out at the stage when they become difficult and not letting them back in until the work is completed. That's a good tactic for any property development manager.

Lastly, remember that if you wish to take construction project management in your own hands, you are fully responsible for the majority of responsibilities enumerated in this chapter. By hiring a professional project/construction manager, you are liberating yourself from these responsibilities.

Chapter 8: Assembling your Construction Team

Chapter Objectives:

**Determining the Manpower you need for your Project

**Finding the Right Person for the Job

**Your Options for Getting Capital

**The Guidelines for Choosing the Best Contractor

As a crucial aspect of the preconstruction phases, you will need to assemble people who can make the project possible. Keep in mind that your responsibilities (as your own construction manager) start from the planning phase.

If you think you are an owner with the time, interest, and skill to manage every area of a significant construction project, then you should be more than capable of choosing your team members. No matter what type of building you have in mind, there will always be 'key tasks' that need to be fulfilled. All construction projects require them, with one person qualified to do each job.

This chapter will discuss the relevant tasks of the construction process along with the people fit for fulfilling them.

Note that these positions and responsibilities were already tackled in the previous chapters. In order for them to make sense to you, the following list will *match* these responsibilities with the most appropriate people in your construction team – beginning with the preconstruction phases of the job:

Financing

Financing is one of the first obstacles you need to overcome for your construction project. If you are reading this book, then you should already have an idea on who to ask for sufficient funding. You could either have the cash in hand, have a wealthy family to support your project, or look for a construction loan. All these are feasible ideas for financing your construction project. With these in mind, here are the people (and institution) that can help you:

Bank – Obtaining a construction loan from the best banks in the United States is not the easiest way to gain funding. However, it has provided construction funds for countless of Americans who never had the luxury of sizable cash reserves. Still, you have to be wary of what loan to avail or else it may end up haunting you in the long run. If you want a short-term loan just until the house realizes its value, then make sure that you have one that you are permitted to pay off early without penalty. Long-term loans have penalties upon early completion because the bank wants to make the maximum amount of money possible even though you only borrowed short term. They may want to inspect the property to ensure that their interests are covered in the event of non-payment. Personally, if you can advise clients to use cash, it's a better way of doing things if they can afford it but if the extent of the renovations means that they end up with a very good housing investment, and then a loan may be their only way to finance the work.

Relatives/Business Partners – Even if friends, relatives, or business partners cannot account for 100% of the funding you require, they can at least contribute to your construction project. Remember to clarify how you're going to repay them. Furthermore, family members may want to become part-owners of your project, so make sure these things are cleared up once you receive the money. If you do have family members involve themselves, make sure that they know that you are the construction project manager and that the only way you can keep control of the budget is if they don't make changes to the specifications which were agreed at the outset. The more people you involve, the more likely they are to insist on changes that really don't add that much value to the project and which frustrate you and your work force.

Yourself – Of course, there is still the possibility of you possessing sufficient funds firsthand. If this is the case, then you have successfully over-come financing as a major obstacle. However, you do need to know that the funds that you have will cover all of the work and work out how you can finance any deficit. Some people use credit cards, but this is a very expensive way of doing it, and the bank may give you an overdraft facility for practically nothing at all, depending upon your reputation with the bank and the amount of time you think you may need this for.

Design and Specifications

As stated in the previous chapters, whatever you do in your construction design, it must conform to the existing building code of the US – specifically the IRC for residential construction projects. Other than remembering the regulations and specifications provided by the IRC, you are free to come up with your own design. For this task, you may need the help of the following:

Stock Plan Books – "Stock" plans and specs found in books are the completed works of architectural firms, freelance architects, and other professionals. The first advantage you will get for acquiring plans from books is that they are almost guaranteed to abide with the building code. Of course, it is also easier to find quality structural designs from these plans. This is cheaper than having a professional architect prepare individual plans but helps you to keep within codes so is a very useful way to go.

Professional Architects – It is no secret that hiring architects cost money, even for residential construction projects. Keep in mind that no two construction projects are exactly alike. This means there is no such thing as one perfect path to use. The advantage of hiring professional architects is that they should know their way around zoning laws, building codes, design options, and so on and so forth. Plus, they should also be willing to accept your input as the owner/construction manager. This makes sure that everyone will be satisfied by the end result. An architect may wish to oversee the work, though it's unlikely. However, if you retain the services of the architect, it's handy when snags come up during the construction as you can get the architect to verify certain measurements on their plans and check with the actual work. However, this does cost money. I prefer to use architects for "green" ventures because there are a lot of unknowns as far as the materials are concerned, and they will have a better idea on what products should be used to conform to code and to look aesthetically pleasing.

DB General Contractors – You can also acquire the design and specs of a project as well as the necessary construction services from a *design-build* (D-B/D/B) *contractor*. It offers the owner a 'singular point of responsibility' that can, in turn, reduce both construction costs and risks. This isn't a bad way to go because the general contractors have their own architects in house and are usually able to provide a full service whereby their staff will actually be responsible for keeping to the timescales that are agreed at the outset.

3D Building Design Software – For non-architects/professional designers, the use of 3D building design software is more on capturing structural ideas rather than finalizing an entire construction plan. Basically, you will still need to be familiar with construction fundamentals to produce a sound construction plan. Most architects today use these 3D architectural software applications to create a complete project plan, so you may want to work closely during the design process. These are similar to those used by the Property Brothers to envisage what rooms will look like with walls taken down and the software is so advanced these days that you really can give a client a clear picture of what to expect once the work is done. Remember that you will need the expertise to use this software and that takes a little bit of time to master, but once you do – it's a super investment, especially if you are thinking of doing this kind of work on a regular basis.

Estimating

You will need an accurate cost estimate, as you'll have to show it to lenders. The entire process of estimating costs should come *after* the completion of the design and specs of the project. Unfortunately, it takes years of experience before one could create accurate estimates of construction projects. There are too many variables in a construction project for you to learn in such a short period of time. This is why you'll need the help of the following people for estimating:

- **The Architect** – Professional architects who are fully involved with your design process should be able to provide you with a clear and often accurate estimate.

- **General Contractor** – If you acquired your project plans from a design-build contractor, they should be able to provide you with accurate estimates of the cost of materials and construction labor. Get them to break down the costs so that you know where you can cut corners if you need to without affecting the quality of the work being done.

Construction Labor

After all the planning, you will need the people who will actually build the structure for you. Of course, the number of people you need for the construction labor depends on the size of your project. Regardless of the size of your labor force, there is always the need for one person to manage the onsite operations – the *foreman* or the *lead carpenter.*

A foreman or lead carpenter oversees and participates in the operations on the construction site. He is in charge of the delivery of construction materials, the functionality of construction equipment, maintaining quality control, and troubleshooting any anomalies. Basically, a lead carpenter should have a technical skill set in terms of construction. Keep in mind that this person is different from the overall *construction manager.* If you want to be your own construction manager but do not have sufficient construction experience in the past, a foreman will fill the gaps for you.

Inspections

During the construction, it is important to have building, plumbing, and electrical inspectors visit your site on regular intervals. These people will make sure your project conforms to the building code. Not only will they ensure that everything works correctly upon completion, they will also provide you with the appropriate actions to take in case they find problems.

You may also ask for their input *during* the design process. It's better to have a complete, working blueprint of the structure rather than to make adjustments later. Remember that these inspectors are trying to help *you,* so be more respectful during the visits. Listen to what they have to say, and you shouldn't have any problems later on.

Supplies

Your suppliers account for around *half* of the entire cost of the project. If you are working with contractors, they will usually handle the bidding for the list of necessary materials. It is also a contractor's job to find the most cost-effective delivery method and acquisition of special orders. Contractors may also help you obtain a line of credit for building supplies.

Observe that there are specific 'key' people that can help you with the most important aspects of a construction project. In addition to those listed above, here is another list of people relevant to a big construction project:

Lawyer

You may ask a lawyer to review a construction contract between you and a prime contractor. Additionally, a lawyer writes a contract on your behalf. A lawyer will help you answer the questions:

**Which party will cover the expenses for design errors/failures?

**Are there any hidden conditions or any identifiable conflicts with the plans and specs?

**What comes next in case your contractor gets fired or is suddenly unable to finish the project?

**Will the contractor compensate for late or delayed projects?

Although a lawyer is often not necessary for small residential constructions and renovations, hiring one will definitely benefit you when it comes to big, expensive projects. Keep in mind that there is no such thing as a 100%-neutral contract. Contracts are *always* written to favor one side -- one way or another.

This should be very easy to do if you have a lawyer friend. Depending on your location, you may also need your lawyer throughout the project.

Take note that there will be more about contracts in chapter 12.

Draftsmen

For most projects, the *draftsmen* are responsible for finalizing the construction blueprints which are required for the necessary permits. If you hired an architect, the architectural firm will usually provide a draftsman for you. They should then provide you with the completed prints. Ask them to have schematics for each of the trades so that they can work to the letter, rather than merely doing their own thing. If you have the schematics in blueprint format, all of your workers will have what they need to do their job properly. This may cost a little extra or you may find a draftsman who can print out triple copies of the blueprints and then mark them up for each trade.

It is also a good idea to collaborate with a draftsman during the design process since they are good with turning rough sketches into feasible structures. Draftsmen will also try to improve your ideas to a point where they can easily and economically be achievable.

Insurance Agent

It is important to consult your insurance agent prior to beginning construction. This is to protect you from any liabilities that may arise from the construction site. In addition, your prime contractor and existing subcontractors must also be duly insured or else any liability incurred by them will be shouldered by you as the owner of the project.

Make sure to ask for insurance certificates upon hiring contractors and subcontractors. To further minimize the risks involved with the entire construction project, you may acquire a *Builder's Risk Insurance* to protect your property under construction. Your prime contractor should also be able to do this for you. This is a good idea as when you are in charge of a building project, it's quite possible that you can damage an adjoining property or that damage can be done to an adjoining property during the renovation process. Of course, it will be accidental, but it's a good idea to have a policy to cover you so that you don't end up paying extra costs that you had not anticipated.

Choosing a Contractor

A lot of medium to large-scale construction projects are handled by general contractors. They are also often referred to as *building contractors, builders,* or *remodeling contractors.* As the owner, it is your job to hire the best possible contractor your budget allows.

Finding a competent building contractor is quite similar to finding a good lawyer, doctor, or accountant. There is no 'catalogue' wherein you can compare and choose from a range of professional contractors. Instead, your best option for comparison is through *word of mouth.*

The best place to start is anyone from your list of friends, colleagues, or neighbors who recently completed a construction project. In addition to observing the completed work firsthand, you can ask them the following questions:

- *How well was the communication between you and the General Contractor?*

- *Did you experience any delays or cost overruns with this particular General Contractor?*

- *How long have you been working with this General Contractor?*

- *Have you experienced working with other contractors? How did this one compare?*

- *How often was the General Contractor on the site? Was there anyone else tasked with the onsite supervision?*

Note that this task is a lot easier if you are working closely with an architect. Professional architects tend to have a list of contractors whom they've worked with in the past. Of course, it is a lot better to build a team with members who are already familiar with each other. It gives each member a good sense of what to expect in terms of quality and work performance.

Of course, it is also important for you to interview a prospective contractor firsthand. To help you identify the competent contactors from the mediocre ones, use the following guide questions:

- *Have you encountered similar projects in the past? If so, how many of them have you completed successfully?*

- *Who exactly will be in charge of the supervision of the construction site?*

- *Who exactly will I be working with when the construction starts?*

- *What do you think is your (or your company's) greatest strength?*

- *What do you suggest is the average cost of this project per square-foot?*

- *Which working conditions do you prefer – cost-plus, negotiated price, competitive bid, etc.?*

- If you are planning a renovation project, ask a contractor, *"What safety measures will you implement to keep the site and its vicinity safe and clean for children?"*

The thing is that when you open up a dialog with a potential contractor, you can tell from his answers to common sense questions such as these whether he is a professional or not. The cowboys in the business are the ones that can't give you straight answers to your questions or who may even avoid giving you any answer at all. Beware of these because it's likely that they will not provide you with the professional service that you are seeking. Stick to those that you get on well with and that can answer questions without beating about the bush.

Lastly, bear in mind that there will always be two sides of the coin. Even if this particular contractor performed very well with previous clients, there is no guarantee that he will be the perfect choice for your particular construction project.

Deciding on contractors, it's important that you know their past work record, their ability to work within timescales and also their ability to follow architectural plans to the letter. If they can't you may be in trouble. You need to work on a regular basis with these people, so make sure that you have a rapport and that you are not afraid of criticizing something straight away if there is a problem, expecting them to rectify it immediately.

A good workforce is worth the time investing in the search because you may continue to do this kind of work and have need of them in the future.

Other than the above approaches, a project owner can also obtain the necessary connections with contractors and architects through bidding. This can be a very rewarding situation and put you in a strong position to go forward with your renovation or constructions plans knowing that you made all the right choices. A lot of local authorities use the bidding system because of its efficiency and this may be an ideal way for you to farm out the work that you have fairly. However, if you are not keen on the bidding system, then by all means do get estimates from several contractors, keeping to the guidelines that the exact work you want quoted for is the same for each contractor and that there are no variances. The trouble with not insisting on that is that some contractors can look very much cheaper than others, but there may be hidden costs, which take their price higher than the other quoting contractors. Watch out for things like this when you use an ordinary estimation system with contractors, as they are very good at hiding detail that a construction manager then has to sort out by comparison

Chapter 9: Guide to Bidding

Chapter Objectives:

**The Basics of Bidding for Construction Projects

**Overviews of Competitive Bidding, Negotiated Bids, Design-Build Bids, and Cost-Plus Bids

The bidding process comes usually after finalizing the detailed plans for your construction project along with the required specifications. Remember that the methods and strategies at play will remain the same regardless if you hired a general contractor or not.

This chapter will help you employ the best bidding strategies for the most cost-efficient construction results.

Soliciting Bids

After collecting and polishing the necessary plans and details of a construction project, the owner should present or publish the required data for *bid solicitation*. This way, the data will be accessible to key people who can turn help with the project (general contractors, construction managers, etc.).

There are government entities and several other service providers who can handle bid solicitation. Of course, a lot of these services come at a price.

Also remember that soliciting bids is often only necessary without the help of an architect or a contractor. With close collaborative work between any of these two, you should be able to have a *negotiated bid* early on. This will be explained shortly after *marking-up the prices*.

Marking-Up the Prices

Never forget that the estimate of possible costs must always be marked up including the *overhead* and *profit*. Your general contractor should be able to provide you with these prices after estimating the costs of the job. Here is a brief clarification for both to avoid confusion:

- **Overhead** – Under overhead are the costs acknowledged by being 'in business' (also known as *soft costs*). To be more specific, this takes into account the following costs:

  o *Bookkeeping and Accounting*

  o *Training*

  o *Legal fees*

  o *Insurance*

  o *Trucking*

  o *Construction Equipment and Tools*

  o *Office Expenses*

- **Profit** – The net profit is calculated once all the costs for finishing the construction project have been paid.

Keep in mind that there are slight differences between companies when it comes to calculating overhead and profit. There are a lot of variables in costs that companies treat differently. This may increase or reduce the costs depending on the needs of your project. For example, while some consider taxes and employee benefits as a hard cost of the project, some put them under overhead. Remember that it is normal for a contractor to seek profit to survive. But as an owner, it is important to spot an overcharging company.

With all these in mind, you should be familiar with the different bidding methods:

Negotiated Bids

There are two ways for a negotiated bid to take place. One, an owner approaches a general contractor first prior to designing the project. In this case, the contractor will then introduce an architect whom he deems qualified for the job. The architect will then try to fine-tune a project to best fit the owner's budget.

In the second way or option, a negotiated bid takes place when the owner approaches the architect first. In which case, the architect will help the owner find the best contractor. After which, the owner will negotiate the price for the project with the contractor (see previous chapter – Choosing a Contractor).

Here are some of the advantages and disadvantages of negotiated bids:

*Although the costs will be transparent throughout the negotiations, it doesn't necessarily mean that you will be getting the best prices due to the lack of competition.

*As an owner, you are guaranteed to have designs that fit your budget. However, the final outcome may turn out to be less creative.

Competitive Bids

In competitive bids, your project data will be accessible to multiple contractors. Once your construction project data becomes public, contractors should be able to place a bid on how much it would take for them to complete the project for you. Naturally, you should be looking for the lowest bidder who can deliver at least an acceptable quality of work.

Again, if you're working closely with an architect in the early design process, he or she may be able to suggest a few names. However, your target should be a reliable company with a reasonable amount of experience.

Here are some of the advantages and disadvantages of competitive bids:

**Although competitive bidding will allow you to find the lowest price for your project, sometimes the lowest bidder will try to compensate by reducing the quality of work.

**While competitive bidding allows you to find the balance of quality and cost-effectiveness, sometimes conflicts arise between the owner, architect, and contractor.

Design-Build Bids

Design-Build bid is essentially a form of negotiated bid from design-build contractors. As stated earlier, design-build contractors offer their involvement from the early design to the construction of a project.

Design-build companies are often run by architects, non-architect contractors, or sometimes, a partnership of the two. These companies have varying price tags as well. When it comes to advantages and disadvantages, design-build bids are essentially the same with negotiated bids.

Cost-Plus Bids

Cost-Plus bids often involve special conditions with the project. This type of bid is more commonly used for home renovations and smaller construction jobs. As far as functions go, this type of bid is perfect for anything that can increase the cost of labor.

Cost-Plus bids usually come in two forms: *cost-plus-a-percentage,* and *cost-plus-a-fixed-fee.*

- **Cost-Plus-a-Percentage** – In cost-plus-a-percentage, the owner pays the contractor for his costs for labor, subcontractors, building materials, as well as a *percentage* for his overhead and profit prices.

- **Cost-Plus-a-Fixed-Fee** – As opposed to cost-plus-a-percentage, a flat fee is paid for a contractor's overhead and profit in cost-plus-a-fixed-fee. In case the owner creates changes regarding the project data, a renegotiation of prices is needed.

Here are some of the advantages and disadvantages for Cost-Plus bids:

**The owner will only pay for the work done at a rate agreed upon with the contractor. However, the owner will shoulder all cost overruns. (Cost-Plus-a-Percentage)

**While the owner still has to shoulder all cost overruns, the contractor is more motivated to stay within the budget and complete the project on time. (Cost-Plus-a-Fixed-Fee)

Bear in mind that if the owner then adds extras to the job, these will need to be noted, as these will not be included in the package. I am adding this because owners tend to do that. They come up with extra ideas during the course of the work that make the costs mountain up and that's not the fault of the contractors or the construction manager, insofar as he is forced to comply with their wishes. However, an experienced construction manager will work within the contingency or the amount that he has allowed and will let clients know in no uncertain terms if the things that they are proposing as changes will have an impact on costs.

When you used fixed bids, you need to know how open a contractor is to extras and the kind of hourly rate that you can expect to pay for these. One client that I had was very difficult in that he decided that he wanted a complex entertainment package added after all the walls had been completed. That was annoying to say the least, since all the decoration had been done and it meant installing wiring behind finished walls. I was able to negotiate for this, but they would have saved a lot of money if they had had the foresight to have sat down and discussed this requirement before the walls were patched up and decorated. Doubling up the work of a contractor because of a change of heart of the owner really can be annoying, but you have to know that your contractor is available to do that work within the given timescale and what it's likely to cost if the customer should decide at the last minute to make changes.

Chapter 10: The Executing Phase

Chapter Objectives:

**What is the 'Executing Phase'?

**The Difference between the Construction Manager and the Project Manager

The Execution Phase requires the bulk of effort among those involved in the construction process. Once the Planning Phase is completed and the contract is signed, purchasing the materials needed and looking for workers commences to start construction. It should be noted that while the result of the construction process is ideally providing the residential structure expected by the client, the process that leads to the end equally matters. This means that executing the project does not only entail implementation of the project plan's structural components but also in managing people to get to that goal.

The execution phase involves the act of accomplishing and doing the work and task at hand for the construction project. In comparison with all the other phases in construction, it is the execution phase that involves the principal actions that are needed in order to successfully finish the bulk of work of the project. So in essence, while the conceptualization and planning were all determined in the first two phases, respectively, the real "action" starts upon start of the third phase – the execution phase. While the first two phases in the construction involved mostly the use of the brain, it is in this third executing phase that the team brings in the muscle to get things done.

In Chapter 4, we mentioned that the project plan is iterative because everyone will always look back into it until the completion of the construction project. This phase is the perfect time to do that because any miscalculation, risks, or mishaps can compromise the general direction of the project.

An important thing to remember when it comes to the executing phase is to always maintain good communication with your construction manager.

Construction Manager vs. Project Manager

Remember that there is a clear distinction between a project manager and a construction manager. Although they may have overlapping responsibilities from time to time, each of them should focus more on separate tasks in order for the entire project to come together.

Basically, a construction manager holds more presence in the *execution phase* of the project. They are directly involved with managing the onsite personnel alongside the foreman. They also make sure the materials are duly delivered and ready to use for the site operations. Additionally, construction managers are responsible for the availability of tools and other necessary equipment, as well as coordinating with engineers, inspectors, clients, and consultants.

On the other hand, a project manager covers much more ground when it comes to the construction project. Aside from being involved with the execution phase of the project, project managers also take part in the administrative aspects such as funding, budgeting, and personnel management.

As far as residential construction and home renovation goes, one person can easily fulfill both jobs depending on the scale of the project. Furthermore, a construction manager *may* fulfill the roles of a project manager for small-scale projects.

Holding a Preconstruction Meeting

A lot of problems in the executing phase arise due to discrepancies in the expectations of your construction team. Small misunderstandings between the owner, the contractor, and the architect may give way to bigger conflicts later on. Quite frankly, being your own construction manager grants you a first row seat in the entire project. This will make it a lot easier to resolve conflicts and misunderstandings within the crew.

Always remember that bad communication is the root of all conflicts in construction. Even if you have a crystal clear blueprint for the project, a lot of things may not look exactly the same way as you pictured it on paper. Furthermore, certain anomalies on the site will definitely be a major inconvenience for anyone involved.

To avoid or fix these conflicts effectively, it is important to have a *preconstruction meeting* to make sure everyone is clear on what to do. Also make sure that you have at least inspected the construction site yourself.

In a preconstruction meeting, everyone involved with the construction project management should attend. They are usually the general contractor, the architect, the owner, the foreman, and the construction manager.

The purpose of the preconstruction meeting is to verify or get clear information on the following:

- The design
- The construction site
- The contract
- Any remodeling issues

If you have hired a lawyer to help you, you might as well invite him over to the preconstruction meeting. Your lawyer should be able to provide direct input regarding specific contract clauses.

Common Remodeling Issues

For remodeling projects, the incursion of your privacy as the owner is a constant risk – especially if you are living with your family on the site. This is why it is important to clarify and set specific rules about what is NOT permitted on the site. Here are some examples of what to discuss extensively with your foreman and contractor:

Tools and materials must always be stored in a secure place away from the reach of children.

The owner's living areas must be clear of any dust and construction debris at all times.

You should also discuss how property damage brought about by the workers or construction equipment is settled.

Throughout the project; are power interruptions to be expected?

Are the site workers welcome to use the family lavatory?

Are the site workers allowed to smoke within the premises?

Although these common remodeling issues have little impact on the work to be done, it might stir up conflicts between the occupants (including the owner) and the construction team. If you have cleared all of this kind of problem up in advance, then those misunderstandings are avoided. I remember working on one project where smoking was not permitted and where one particular workman spent most of his time at the back of the house doing nothing while he had a cigarette. As long as your price allows for this kind of delay, you will be okay, but if you can choose a non-smoking contractor in circumstances such as this, you will get more work from them in a shorter time frame and upset no one.

The thing is that this is going to be someone's home and they may have strong views about certain elements. Getting these all cleared up at the beginning is the best way forward since it stops all misunderstandings in their tracks and means that you are working within the client's guidelines from the word "go." You may also ask them if there is any of the work that they wish to do or if they have particular items that they want included in the renovation. One couple I worked for had a stained glass window they wanted to incorporate and we managed to get a double glazed unit made using that, so that it stayed on code and also gave them the decorative effect that they wanted.

One thing that should be borne in mind is when the Project Manager and the Construction Manager role are taken by one person who believes that they can take on both roles adequately. In the case of individuals this is often the case, which is why we have referred to construction managers throughout this book. However, in a firm, this would be different.

If you do decide to take on both roles, that places extra strain upon you and you must be prepared to work with it. If you are doing a house for yourself and your family and you take on this role, remember that during the course of the renovation, the family will still expect you to perform your role within that family and this is liable to cause some friction. The worry of construction will eat away at your nighttime hours. You will find that you are unable to concentrate on more than the house and it's always a good idea at the end of the job to get away from it all with the family and enjoy time together.

The strain that this can put on a family is enormous. If you are calm person and able to do this without the strain and who has great organization abilities, you may find that you perform the job with very little trouble at all, but remember that you are personally invested because it's your home. That adds pressure to the situation that would not otherwise be there were you working for a client.

One of the most impressive Construction Manager/Project Manager people that I have ever encountered was a woman. Her husband was able to take on a lot of her roles for her during the time of the construction, but she was extremely organized, personable with the staff and able to get great discounts on the items used within the house. She was also able to cut through the paperwork quickly and had links with people in the planning department and a brother who was an architect. Between them, they really did do a first rate job and the job came out on budget and very professionally finished. You can't help but be impressed by people who take on the dual role and those that do this successfully need the following attributes:

- Patience,
- Understanding
- Strong Character
- Great organization ability
- Ability to sort out problems as they occur

Chapter 11: The Controlling Phase

Chapter Objectives:

**The Importance of the Controlling Phase*

The Controlling Phase occurs at a later time after the Execution Phase started. This is because the Controlling Phase has three primary functions: to make sure that the work dome satisfies what is stated in the project plan, to ensure that that different milestone in the construction project is done with quality as expected, and to integrate changes in the project plan when needed.

We mentioned that the project plan is the backbone of every construction project. However, it is not foolproof. First, the Controlling Phase sets the standards of quality that the construction project should have. In view of the project plan, both execution and the resulting structure should not fall below the expected quality. If it happens that the quality of the result is way below than what is specified in the project plan, changes should be made in order for the result and the plan to be aligned.

Second, the Execution Phase is when the Project Manager's skills are tested. During the Controlling Phase, the Project Manager's performance is evaluated in terms of his ability to fulfill the different roles he is supposed to fulfill. In Chapter 1, we laid out some of the responsibilities and the accountabilities of the Project Manager.

Third, there are instances where changes are not made during the Execution Phase as a result of testing in the Controlling Phase (cue: Quality Control). Instead, the changes are done on the project plan itself. While that sound worrisome especially in time-bound projects, it can happen, and the price to be paid will not necessarily cost major construction adjustments. This explains why the Controlling Phase is done almost simultaneously with the Execution Phase. So what drives changes to the project plan?

First, the client might issue a change order specifying the components of the plan that needs to be changed. This is possible, but it comes with consequences: the client will pay more money to accommodate the changes, and the entire project itself might require a different deadline. There are times though when a client's request seems to be too far off from the project plan. In this case, the Project Manager comes in to analyze everything and to help the client make an informed decision. This takes us to the second factor that causes a project plan to change.

When a client issues a change order, the Project Manager is in charge of making such change. Thus, the second factor deals with how the project plan is changed in itself. As expected, if the Project Manager executes change, he is responsible for relaying the modifications to everyone involved in the project. This way, the risks associated with misinformation or the lack thereof can be avoided. Both the changes requested for by the client and executed by the Project Manager are represented by a single phrase: integrated change control.

Problems with integrated change control

The potential problems that can occur with this kind of change are that the change has to fit with planning permissions. You can't change things on a whim and expect to get away with it. Fortunately, most property owners let the builders do the main structural work and leave them to it. However, it has been known for changes to be requested which don't meet the original plans. Things that come to mind instantly are beams. People are okay with the idea of a steel beam being inserted to secure the ceiling structure when walls are taken away, but these have to meet stringent guidelines. Often when the client sees the beams, they are a little baffled by them and want changes. If you are changing things, which require permission, this will slow down the whole procedure and you need to make your clients aware of that.

Sometimes, boxing these in so that they are not so apparent may be the answer. In one series of the Property Brothers, there was a supporting post that could not be removed without substantial permission and alteration to the actual structure of the building, which would have cost the family a fortune. Instead of doing that, they were clever enough to come up with a design whereby that post was not noticeable. The clients were satisfied. The building codes were not breached and the budget was not affected.

Being in charge of the project, if you can use software to show the client what the property will look like even though some potential eyesore appears to be on the scene midway through the renovation, you can sometimes persuade clients to go along with your ideas, putting trust in what you say and what you know you can produce, within the parameters of the original schedule of work but disguised sufficiently to make them work within the scheme that the homeowner wants.

Do not agree to every change put forward. If you do, you will regret it. As we have said previously, people can be fickle when it comes to home renovations and within a week or two have completely forgotten that they asked you to do that change anyway. Talk your way around it if you think it will affect costs, time scale for finishing and permits.

Chapter 12: The Closing Phase

Chapter Objectives:

**What is the Closing Phase and why is it Necessary?

**The 9 Steps for Construction Project Management (PMBROK)

Simply put, the Closing Phase is a culmination of a construction project. This phase includes various procedures that inform the client of a completed job. But even before a project is declared complete, the Project Manager will have to go through one last stage of evaluation of the tasks, reviewing receipts, filling up necessary paperwork, and finally fulfilling the closing requests made by the client. The Closing Phase is a short process in contrast to the first five phases. Once a project is deemed complete, the client takes over.

Note: The Project Management Body of Knowledge (PMBOK)

The different phases discussed in this book are similar to the nine project management areas stipulated under PMBOK. This means that the five phases discussed in the previous chapters are a representation of a more comprehensive set of knowledge that is embodied in a standard and international literature. Under PMBROK, the nine steps towards construction project management are as follows:

- Integration
- Scope
- Time
- Cost
- Quality

- Human Resource

- Communication

- Risk

- Procurement

You can easily tell where each of the five phases fall given the areas above. Because there are a lot of areas, it is easier and more practical to approach the project management process in the context of an ongoing project and with a hands-on point of view. Now that we've been through the different phases and areas in construction project management, let's wrap up our discussion by focusing one integral component of construction – the paper that binds everything that is done in construction: the contract.

Before doing that, however, your final paperwork should be something that you can back up and explain to a client. For example, if there are extras, you need to provide the works order from them that says that they are prepared to bear the brunt of the extra cost of certain items. Thus keep your paperwork in good order at all times. On your chart of budget costs, mark extras in another color so that you know these are items the client agreed to pay for. You should be able to show your complete picture of the renovation to the client's satisfaction and if you have kept meticulous details of everything, this won't be that hard to do.

Show them the different agreements that you had and alterations to the drawings that were the original drawings. Show them extra costs in involving the appropriate authority to come and check things over. On Property Brothers, they even furnish the house to the client's requirements having taken brief details on the kind of style that the family likes. If you are going to go this far, then make sure that you have all the necessary paperwork ready and that you have kept your clients informed every step of the way. That way, there are no misunderstandings at the last minute on what things cost.

Try to show your client some form of saving as well because that always makes them happy and gives them a little cash to spend on something nice for their new home. The 35 per cent contingency may not have been spent and there's nothing quite as good in the closing stages as having the bill come out on target and being told that the contingency was not touched.

If you have been clever during the course of the renovation, you may find that what happens is that you can make small savings throughout the job without cutting down on the quality of the items used. These all add up and help to make the final tallying up more satisfying for the client and for you. It certainly is satisfying being able to finish a job under budget.

Chapter 13: Things that Will Help You in Your Career

Although you probably bought this book because you have decided to become a Construction overseer in some capacity or other, there is courses that you can take that will help you with your career. The more that you know about real estate in your area, the better. This helps you to see the potential profit that can be made on a home but it also keeps you informed of property trends. If you can take a course in this locally, this really will help you to be able to deal with the day to day running of projects on a very realistic basis.

Another project worthwhile learning about is using the software that makes the home look the way it will look when it is finished. It's not enough to just buy the software. Learn from someone who is proficient at using it because then you can come up with so many variations of ideas that will work just as well for the client and charge them for it as well as part of the overseeing of the project itself.

Brush up on your management skills and learn how to deal with day to day problems because all of this is part and parcel of the job. Keep yourself apprised of new products as and when they come onto the market, because viable alternatives may make a project cheaper but also ecologically sounder. If you do have the time to study, it's worthwhile because you may come across projects that give you particular difficulties that can be overcome smoothly and efficiently by use of new products on the market. You will also need to know who supplies them and who installs them and at what cost.

People are getting to be a lot more Earth friendly and "green" and if you can keep up to date on the schematics for solar systems and geothermic energy these are useful to your trade. These kinds of systems provide energy at a much lower cost than normal running costs of a home, thus making the home more economical to run and long term a better investment than homes that have no such features.

Grants and Other Government allowances

You need to keep appraised of these as tax incentives may be offered to your clients if they keep their home repairs in compliance with government regulations for grants. These may be available for houses where an improvement in efficiency is installed or will be achieved because of the renovation. In cases like this, you normally need to have agreement to the price quoted for the work in advance and the customer may have to wait until declaring their taxes to get a tax credit, but this can make a whole world of difference to the job that you perform and you may be able to offer people cheaper alternatives because of the tax incentives given.

You also need to keep up to date on new paints, finishes and trends in kitchens and bathrooms because these are areas, which will invariably be changed by homeowners. Homeowners are not keen on using kitchens which are dated and which have been used by others. As a project manager, gather information – gather samples – gather prices and never be afraid to offer your client an alternative finish because often there is little difference between that which you offer with a discount and that is on their wish list. There really isn't much in it at all but you can save your client a fortune and keep your suppliers happy at the same time.

One area to look out for is when tilers and floor layers try to sell you products that they get through the trade. It is a better idea that you have a trading account yourself and take all the profit from the prices that you are given. Hardwood flooring and items such as this can be costly, but if you have already negotiated a deal on different floorings locally, you can offer clients alternatives that make them feel that they are part of the renovation process and are getting good value. Then employ your own workforce to lay the floors, knowing that you will get consistent results each time and don't have to rely upon independent contractors for this part of the work.

Learn who architects recommend as contractors and how long they have been working with that particular contractor. These are all valuable contacts for you and you need to be able to offer alternative packages to your homeowners, so the more reliable workforce you can employ, the more likely you are to do this. Know your planning department and let them get to know you. This is important to your job because you will know which are the experts on which particular kind of work and will be able to get in touch with them straight away when you need them instead of sitting on the end of the line waiting for someone else to direct you.

As a property or construction overseer, you have enough on your plate without making things more complex than they need to be. Have a set of regulations applicable to your area so that you know that your building complies in every way possible. There is a trend now for tiny homes and you may be asked to work on one of these. Be aware of what the rules are as often these are not viable residences since they fall outside the scope of building codes.

To be good at your job, you need to know so much information but if you are information orientated, this could be the perfect job for you. Some people are and they make a very good job of Project management in the area of homebuilding or home renovations. They have the contacts. They are not fazed by client's requirements and are flexible in their approach to home building. They know the rules and know how to bend them a little to suit a particular environment. For example, many people want glass in huge quantities in their homes today as this provides heat and light and can also be used to help keep the temperature of a room constant. Look into your local glass suppliers and keep appraised of what they can provide.

Learn where to get off the shelf goods and know the standard sizes. Learn also how much carpenters charge for bespoke items. Don't rule them out because of cost as some clients really do want bespoke and are more than willing to pay for it, particularly in traditional houses where the aesthetics are important. The thing is that in the trade you are in, you need to know all of the suppliers and all of the contractors in your area and have an idea of how cost effective they are. Knowing products will also give you an edge because it enables you to suggest certain "green" products to your clients that actually go a long way to meeting their needs. With so many new forms of heating, get to know what's available locally and work out the most pleasing for your contract. If the property has a lot of ground, then you have the possibility of including a heating system that takes its main heat from the earth around the house and that's beneficial long term because it will save your client a lot of costs on utilities.

Your architect will be able to give you a lot of information and can be asked to include "green" elements in his design so that you don't have to do all the legwork. Once the drawings are done, you will know the kind of products that are being suggested and can look to improve upon them keeping the property in the same lines as suggested by the architect but using products that are easier to use and that cost less in manpower to actually use.

Ideas here include insulation that is sprayed into cavities instead of insulation that takes many people to put in place. There are also insulation products worth considering for cavity walls and for ceilings. Be aware of what they are. When people are building or renovating in this day and age, they are looking for long-term value. It may cost them a little more now, but think of the long-term benefits that they will derive from those products. By keeping yourself aware of what's new, you offer your clients something special that can't be tailored by people who haven't had the foresight to actually look into them as viable propositions.

When your reputation spreads, you may find yourself having more work than you care to deal with but at least you will leave behind you a trail of quality work which will help you to find more lucrative work in the future and that's what the building trade is all about.

Chapter 14: The Role Effective Communication Plays in the Success of Construction Project Management

Chapter Objectives:

**Why the need to communicate effectively?*

**Common Kinds of Communication*

Why the need to communicate effectively?

Projects will never be as successful if members in this team are not able to work harmoniously with each other and there are constant misunderstandings among the people who comprise these groups. In order for specific goals and tasks indicated in projects to be efficiently carried out, the team must have cooperation; the team must possess effective teamwork. And in order to have this agreeable nature within the group, all team members must be able to communicate with other members of the project team in a manner that gets their message across in an effective manner.

Communication is crucial in project management, and especially when dealt with construction projects where the pressures come from all directions. Pressures from the client and the owners and other team members to meet deadlines. The last thing you need is to add to this stress by having problems with communication within the team.

Getting the right rapport in the work place or the construction site to encourage successful communication among team members does not have to be a difficult task. The first thing project leaders and managers must do is to create trust and respect within the team. Without these two, others will find it hard to listen to their colleagues and maybe even will not find the need to talk to their coworkers.

Teach your team to be confident speakers, being able to voice out their minds in the most polite and courteous way possible and in well suited and appropriate situations.

Imagine if in your team no one bothers to care enough for the project to voice out concerns. Other members will have to assume in everything and assumptions often lead to misunderstandings and mistakes. Establish a way for your team to be able to communicate properly within the work place, this will make your working environment more enjoyable and would save you the trouble of fixing mistakes caused by simple misunderstandings.

Common Kinds of Communication

There are many different methods for communication to take place. In the construction project management setting, we have already emphasized the need for members to have good communication lines among each other. Team members need to frequently inform one another on the latest progress and updates in their project. Members can take advantage of the modern technology in order to make tasks a lot easier for everyone involved in the common goal and also to be assured of rapid and precise communication among team members.

Common modern communication technologies include electronic mail, chat and video conference services such as FB messenger and Skype, the use of short message services (SMS) or text messaging via cellular phones and tablets, document sharing services via the cloud such as Dropbox, Google share, and iCloud.

More advanced means of communication can include the use of construction program management software specifically designed for use in the construction industry. More details on these kinds of tools and computer software will be discussed a little further along this book. Meanwhile, this chapter emphasizes the importance of good communication within a project team and each one involved in this business should learn to value this tool more. This well may be the lifeline that keeps your business and the industry alive, since after all construction is indeed a business that involves the realization of thoughts and ideas into tangible solid structures that were once just figments of human imaginations. For a group of people to effectively construct this idea coming from a single person requires effective communication indeed.

Chapter 15: The Importance of Proper and Systematic Documentation of the Construction Project Management

Chapter Objectives:

**To Know and Appreciate the Usefulness of Proper Documentation in Construction Project Management

** To Know Typical Methods and Techniques for Making and Filing Records used in the Construction Project Management

**To Know the Basic List of Documents that should be kept for Construction Project Management Documentation

Usefulness of Proper Documentation in Construction Project Management

The proper documentation of the entire construction project as well as its management is of primary importance because this not only keeps the work in a systematic and more organized condition but also allows the company or other users to utilize the records in future situations. It is very important that the documentation be made as detailed as possible because one can never tell when this information can become extremely utile.

While the demands and settings of a certain construction project may be very different from all other projects, it is still highly necessary that project managers establish and follow a systematic method of keeping all records of the activities done during construction. This systematic and orderly method of record keeping contributes to the efficiency of the project management. Also, this method is very useful when observed by large scale businesses that frequently perform construction projects. With a complete record of all its current and past projects, the company saves much money by cutting spending

127

used for cost estimation, this also makes the work load a lot less burdensome for project managers as well as the project team because they already have records of previous projects and they can use this as reference for making sure their current projects do not fail to impress their clients.

Another advantage of having and practicing an orderly technique in record keeping even prior to the start of any project is that it allows for the easy preparation and maintenance of the work as it gradually develops. This technique will also help immeasurably in the furnishing of the final contract records that is a requirement upon the successful culmination of the project. Being able to start with proper record keeping during the initial stages of the project will save the project leaders a great deal of trouble and stress at the end of the contract, because he or she has one less worry to fuss about, anyone in the project team (especially the Project Manager) will find this help extremely convenient especially during the finalization of the project where he or she is also required to provide piles and piles of other paper works for both the contractor and the client.

The characteristic of a successful documentation scheme in construction project management involves having all the calculations and measurements supporting payments for materials, equipment, tools, labor fees, and other resources in the project to be highly accurate and that paper works for all these purchasing actions are complete. The documentation and records should be to a sufficient degree detailed and maintained in a way that will be acceptable to an inspection of the accounting procedures and records by a trained accountant or certified public accountant. Upon close, methodological and careful examination or review of the status of the budget, the records should be in a decipherable condition and in an easily perceptible manner that would allow professional auditors to easily understand and analyze the paper works.

This documentation is not only for the benefit of professional auditors, but the presentation of the records must also be in a fashion that would enable even an individual who barely has any background on the project to understand what they represent. The documentation should be arranged with the thought in mind that the output should be able to stand alone without the need for anyone else to explain all its contents just so the future user can understand it. Remember that a huge part of the reason why we keep documentations of construction projects is because we want to be able to make it serve its purpose as possible reference for future projects who want to learn from the experiences of our currently completed project.

Part of effective documentation is the ability to keep all original receipts and notes used in the duration of the project. In fact it is often advocated that these original transaction accounts such as purchasing receipts, pay slips, notes used on field, minutes of meetings within the construction site personnel and among the client, owners and Project Manager should all be filed and included in the documentation and should be arranged in a manner that it can be kept as basic reference document. It is for this simple reason that the writing of field notes, minutes and other arbitrary details that pertains to anything that concerns the project should always be done in acceptable paper, never consider documenting using scratch papers. Even in these minute details, every member of the project team should learn to practice professional actions. Consequently, do try to avoid transcribing these original documents into final record form, doing so would greatly encourage the possibility for errors and the keeping of false information. Not to mention the unneeded additional spending due to the need to produce copies of these documents. It is both wasteful and not highly reliable.

It is the responsibility of every member of the project team to make certain that notes are carefully and correctly written, and equally important that the information is complete and filled with all necessary information.

In the documentation of communications done using electronic mail or facsimile machines, it is not unusual for information to be conveyed and exchanged in this modern manner. But it is recommended that for documentation and book keeping purposes, original copies of these documents should also follow the information exchange. In other words, upon communicating using these convenient methods, the project team member should always follow the contact up with original copies of all these documents.

Typical Methods and Techniques for Making and Filing Records used in the Construction Project Management

There are correct means of creating, filing and storing notes used during the progress of construction both on and off site. The following are simply suggestions on what should be followed with adequate caution to ensure effective documentation:

1. Every note made should always have in them inscribed the date upon which they were written as well as the initials, signature or complete name with role in the project (if possible) of the individual who created the note.
2. Every note should include the date when the phases of work have been completed successfully, the information about the person who created the note (initials, signature, name, position), the initials of the person who analyzed and examined the quantities mentioned, the dates when of the computation of the quantities, the dates when the computations were subsequently checked, the place where the work was performed and all the corresponding necessary details.
3. Whenever notes used on field are utilized as a kind of receipt to denote the payment to a certain individual, the date should always be included as well as the initials of the person, the person verifying the payment exchange

4. It is recommended that the notes and documentation used in the field be numbered orderly and labeled in order to avoid losing them and to aid in tracking these activities.

5. Notes and basic documents should be written in a clear and neat manner where handwriting is legible and not too congested on paper and with enough detail so as to be easily understood.

Basic List of Documents that should be kept for Construction Project Management Documentation

One of the biggest reasons why one has to document the progress of a construction project is to be able to avoid all the complicated and unnecessary legal problems that may arise when disputes may occur. Also to be able to provide hard copies of the documents should the client, contractor or anyone else requires these documents. The following are some of the basic documents that the Project Manager should file during the course of the construction project:

1. Construction Contract – This document lays out all the basic initial conditions agreed upon before the initiation of the construction. The roles of corresponding parties should also be detailed in this document.

2. Purchase Orders – These papers indicate the date and details of purchases made. This document is especially useful when following up on delayed orders or checking up on the accuracy of delivered items or goods.

3. Bid Documents – This could help support cost estimates indicated in the project proposal as well as back up budget allocation and help in the accounting of resources.

4. Log of Schedule – An updated schedule of work done during the duration of the project will allow for easy monitoring of the

progress of the project. In the same manner, this will also enable both the client and contractors to understand the reason behind any unexpected delays.

5, Project Diaries – Project Managers are highly recommended to keep a journal that is filled with daily records concerning the progress of the project. Additional information that may be useful additions to the diary are details on the attendance of personnel and subcontractors present on site, the current weather condition, any sudden or planned visits by third parties, deliveries of vital materials, significant conversations, finding out new information about the site, such as never before explored hidden conditions of the site and disagreements between the concurred upon plans and breaking out of conflicts, and all other happenings that may be worthy of notice. In special instances when project conflict or hidden conditions or delays should happen, the Project Manager must file a different report that requires the discovery and proper management of the specific problem.

6. Change Orders and Change Order Logs – It is almost unavoidable for one project not to have one or at least one change in order. This inconvenience may further cause a negative impact on the progress of the project. It is therefore not only wise but useful to keep records of these change orders in order to manage follow ups.

7. Design Documents – These documents include original and modified plans, their characteristics and technical specifications, drawings and other requests. Everything that has anything to do with the design of the project and its evolution on how it came to be should always be secured.

8. Project Correspondence – All forms of communication that has anything to do with the project should be kept safe and filed. This is for further reference when one needs to counter check on certain issues or clarification.

9. Job Cost Reports and Estimates – It is good accounting practice to create a report that tabulates the actual cost of any item procured alongside their estimated costs. This technique is especially useful, and often times required, for large scale projects where the auditing of purchases and budget remaining and preparation of financial reports become a more complicated and demanding task. Keeping records of these reports are also useful when monitoring real time budget and identifying the reasons behind possible discrepancies in budget details.

10. Financial Statements – These statements ensure that the finances of the project are current and well accounted for. These statements allow transparency in the work place and make the workers better able to trust the system, giving them the motivation to do better at work.

11. Employee Payroll Records – For large scale projects, a huge percentage in the total budget is often designated for salaries of the human work force. Keeping records of payroll records of the project personnel will come handy when it comes to proper accounting of budget.

12. Videos and Photographs – In order to have a visual documentation that tracks the progress of the project, videos and photographs that have time stamps and dates would serve to be very useful. These resources can also be used in meetings with the client and the contractor, to show them evidences of how the goals and aims of the project is slowly being followed.

13. Miscellaneous Documents – These include meeting minutes, the notes obtained during field and construction on site visits. Other documents that you may find useful can also be filed under this sector for documentation.

Chapter 16: Construction Project Management Software and Tools

Chapter Objectives:

**Basic Concepts Regarding Construction Project Management Software*

**Examples of Top Construction Project Management Software*

Basic Concepts Regarding Construction Project Management Software

The increased interest in construction for the recent years have seen a significant increase in the rise of hundreds of new structures, buildings (both private and public) and other infrastructures all across the globe. The booming construction industry have also increased employment in this field and provided work to a countless many. Along with these advancements in the construction industry, it is also worthy to mention that other factors that have an indirect or direct link to the industry have also benefited from this increase. Examples of these contributing factors are commercial industries that provide and supply for these construction materials and basic tools, as well as those producing and selling the construction equipment. Another branch of commerce that has also been benefiting from the increased interest in construction is the computer and programming industry that has tapped into the construction industry. Over the years, there has been an increase in the number of technological tools that aimed to make the management of construction projects more organized, systematic, easily managed and less prone to errors due to estimation and calculation mistakes. More and more software for this application are being developed and the supply for this software will undoubtedly continue to grow so long as the market continues to demand for these products.

You will be shocked in the number of software that has been developed for the particular purpose of enabling the use of computers for the managing of affairs related to the construction. A lot have been constantly being upgraded and made even "better with additional premium features" so as to become more competitive than the other well recognized software built for the same core purpose.

I have been able to scout through the resources available for construction project management, and the following list of software I will present to you will be briefly described along with their user reviews.

Examples of Top Construction Project Management Software

1. Procore: The Cloud Based Construction Software – This is among the top software being used by individuals or groups involved in construction projects. This is developed by the Procore Technologies, Inc. and has been dubbed as the most commonly used management software for a construction project setting. The cloud based nature of this software promises high security but simple platform to work on. The interface is user friendly with its simple one page project dashboard that allows the users to handle more than one project at a time and also to keep the tabs on their progress and status. This software is jam packed with useful features which makes it very easy to see why this has become a favorite tool for most of the individuals involved in construction project management.

Companies who use this technology have seen the difference in their efficiency and ability to answer to particular concerns in their construction project. These advantages can be achieved through Procore's feature of being able to economically contour and easily circulate communications and documentations within the project.

This software is also handy for individuals who simply want to manage their projects using the convenience of their portable devices hooked into the internet. Project documents that you can work on in the Procore software include contracts, schedules, drawings, submittals and so much more.

2. WorkflowMax: a Xero Product – This software allows its users to carry out actions that would help in the management of his or her job, invoice and time management. The features included in this software include access to sales leads, initiation, implementation, closing and billing phases of the project. This software can be very useful for subcontractors in the project management such as engineers, architects, surveyors and all other construction professionals.

3. BuildTools – This software, constructed and managed by a private company situated in Minneapolis, United States of America, is pretty basic in giving you simple features that you might need, without all the other complicated platforms that you might just end up not using. Working with a web-based platform, it allows users to manage their communication with other members of the project team or anyone not involved in the team. Other features include being able to check and see your schedule, the budget, tasks and other documents. Your information in this software can only be accessed if you have connection to the internet.

4. Co-construct – This is another web-based construction project management software which is specifically designed for remodelers, builders of custom designs and firms responsible for constructing designs. The characteristics of this construction tool are that the platform relies how it functions on the most frequent challenges that users face. It has basic schedule management features, such as calendars, that never forget to remind you of impending deadlines. It is a great communication tool that updates its users as soon as one user has input information for everyone in the team to read.

5. BuilderTREND – This tool is also cloud-based, which means that without internet connection the user will not be able to gain access to its full features. This software has received recognition as a remodeler project management software. The BuilderTREND allows the users to conduct processes before sale such ass proposal generation, lead management, and bid management. Organizing tools such as lead management, bid management and proposal generation can provide users with processes that happen before official sale processes. Management functions involving documents management and change orders.

6. PayPanther – This software brags of being a powerful tool that allows you to have it all in just one simple program. The developer promises to help you use almost the entirety of your time to your work in the construction site rather than focusing so much of it being anxious about the management of the supplies and transport of resources in your construction project. The software has put together varied functionalities such as invoicing, project management, and tracking and bound them all up in the neat package of the PayPanther. The website based software is promoted to be very easy to use and very convenient as well because you are saved the hassle of having to connect to 6 different websites just to have all your tasks done. With the PayPanther, you can do so much more with so much less. You are able to efficiently manage your affairs, save resources and time and save the worry of having to manage different accounts and entries in different software.

7. Synchro Software – Created by Synchro Ltd. for the use of professionals, individuals or businesses who work in the construction industry. Users have especially found the 4D virtual simulation of construction feature of the software which allows the users to see a software generated prototype of his or her design. This advanced feature allows users to get a simulated picture of his or her work and grants him or her the advantage of being able to correct possible errors in the design and improve the output before finalizing with construction. This feature allows users to save cost and time resolving issues before construction could even take its course.

With the positive outlook in the status of the construction industry in the world, and as more and more news on the improvement of the world economy fill our TV screens and newspapers. Companies and professionals as well as businesses who are in the construction industry will find better outlooks in the next years ahead. These tools and software will undeniably make getting involved in this construction industry all the more fun and convenient.

Chapter 17: All about the Contract

Chapter Objectives:

**When is a Contract Necessary?*

**What should be Included in a Construction Contract?*

**How a Contract is processed in a Construction Project*

Not every construction project requires a contract. In Chapter 2, we mentioned that there are two sources of a construction project: internal and external. An internal construction project does not necessarily involve writing and signing a contract. Typically, it involves the top management reviewing the proposal written by the Project Manager and giving a formal signal for the construction to start. Residential real estate developers often follow this flow when they acquire land and want to turn it into a residential complex.

On the other hand, a project that comes from the outside definitely merits a contract. The contract is drafted, delivered to the client, and signed by parties in agreement right when an approval is given to the project proposal or the project plan. It is possible that a contract will undergo revisions before a construction project finally begins. So what should be under a contract?

The following areas should be covered in a construction contract:

Specifics of the construction

This helps you considerably because if all the details and the blueprint are included in the contract there can be no arguments at the end that you did not provide the service you offered a client. Thus, make your contract as detailed as you possibly can to protect you and to protect the client.

Quality standard

When you agree with a client on the quality of items that will be used, you give them assurances but you also protect yourself.

Warranty of the builder

The warranty of the builder also gives your client more confidence and the warranty needs to be given upon completion of the home. This will usually include a set period, during which the client can complain about snagging items, or items that happen over a period of time. This can include settlement cracks and items that may be expected at the end of a large renovation. The client will feel better to know that this will be dealt with in a timely manner and that the builder is aware of his obligation to the client and is willing to uphold it. This confidence that a homeowner gets from the part of the contract that deals with quality and warranty are particularly interesting from a client's point of view.

Conflict resolution

In the Contract, you need some set format for dealing with any problems that arise out of disputes. If you have kept all of your paperwork and records, this should not be a problem and conflicts can be looked over by an independent person such as your lawyer if it comes to an argument. However, most conflicts are dealt with by you and should give fairness to the client. Having some kind of remark in the contract about the timely resolution of conflict should be sufficient to give the client confidence.

Timeline of the construction

This is a very important part of the contract and the client may insist that there are penalties if the property is not completed on time. You do need to make sure that there is a clause within this that says that this is dependent upon suppliers being able to supply special orders on time, as often suppliers let you down at the last minute which is outside of your control.

Contract price

When you add the contract price, the client needs to know if this includes taxes. They also need to know exactly what work this covers, hence the blueprint. Thus, when they alter the contract with instruction notes of changes, you have sufficient detail to be able to justify the change in price.

Construction budget

This part of the contract should show the amount you anticipate the job costing plus the 35 percent contingency and this should always be marked as a contingency to be used in the event of unforeseen costs. The client will be very agreeable to that because they are usually aware that there will be some small costs that cannot be quoted for at the time of the original contract, but that come up as the house is stripped and things are discovered which were not previously anticipated. By showing this, you are showing prudence and homeowners appreciate that. They are also being made aware that the 35 percent is the only contingency on the job and thus they should restrict the amount of changes that they impose because the contingency money will only stretch so far and is intended for emergency costs which were unknown at the time of writing the contract. Make it clear that if this is not used, it will be refunded. That makes clients very happy. You also need to keep notes of everything that you spend within that contingency so that you can justify your final bill without problems. Keeping the client fully informed as and when you find something is a good move because they can see it and they can anticipate the cost and are not left in the dark until the last moment.

Inspection guidelines

This section of the contract refers to work that needs to be to code and for which certification is required. It gives the client a lot of confidence when the correct inspections are made and noted in the contract and they are given the correct certification after the job is finished from each of the trades that have that restriction placed on the work that they do.

Pertinent notes or clauses

Each of the areas above is self-explanatory and is flexible. Some construction firms add special areas in the contract. Then again, it's entirely up to the circumstances of the construction project and the client's preferences. You may have to add in this area how the work may finish at a later date if the homeowner decides to change plans and that this will be beyond the control of the Construction Manager if the client is insistent upon changes that were not anticipated at the time of drawing up the contract.

A Very Important Note

Perhaps the most important function of the contract is legitimizing the authority of the Project Manager. It should be noted that as in other cases requiring a binding document, a contract involving a construction project is the basis for the Project Manager's decisions. However, note that the areas specified above are not ideal. Instead, they only represent the common areas found in construction contracts, so it should not be taken as an encompassing tool. The best course for every Project Manager or construction firm and client is to seek legal advice involving formal agreements. Being a project manager comes with so many different duties that you really do need to write down a list of the things that you will be expected to take on so that you can also work out whether it's worth it or whether you should employ a construction project manager that you trust to do the work in the way that you want it to be done. Sometimes, you can work with your architect's help and work things out yourself, but you must be organized and willing to be there to put things right as and when things start to go awry.

Chapter 18: Managing Home Renovations

Chapter Objectives:

**Step-by-step guide for Managing Home Renovations*

**The Differences between Residential Construction and Home Renovation*

From the Project Manager's point of view, residential construction and home renovation are practically the same with just a few basic changes. The latter is obviously less extensive since the project is not starting from scratch. However, you need to understand that renovation still involves the three basic phases: estimating, planning and scheduling.

Home renovations are usually done due to a variety of reasons. Aside from the obvious space and aesthetic demands of the homeowner, a renovation can also lead to more efficient plumbing, energy efficiency and improved comfort. House value improvement is also an added bonus, allowing residents to increase their price of their residence in the event of a sale.

Here's a step-by-step process overview on managing home renovations.

Step 1: Assessment and Data Gathering

During this stage, the Project Managers aims to understand what needs to be renovated and the extent of the work involved. It's important to note that residential construction renovation still involves paperwork, specifically altering any documents connected to the building. A PM would need to take into account the legal repercussions of the change in the home's plan.

A major difference between residential construction and renovation is that the former starts from scratch. This means that the PM only needs to follow the plan when it comes to plumbing, electrical wirings, etc. During a renovation however, the changes must be made without disturbing the original layout of the home's wirings. This doesn't just refer to the plumbing and electricity but also to the bear-loading walls, size, structural inconsistencies, finishes and more. Project Managers are advised to learn more about the resident's preferences to help them create a list of future jobs.

Step 2: Listing the Jobs that need to be done

Once you've gathered sufficient data, it's time to figure out exactly what needs to be done to successfully complete the renovation. Much like with Residential Construction, you need to start from the bottom and work your way to the jobs needed as the renovation is finished. This stage is also used to estimate the possible cost of the job using stick or unit estimating. According to a homebuilders association, home renovations must be prioritized by the homeowner. Any addition or changes should be grouped accordingly: urgent, discretionary and wish list. Urgent means that the item is necessary, discretionary is optional but adds value to the home and wish list involves personal preferences like a gym or a meditation room.

Step 3: Finding Contractors for the Job

Unlike Residential Constructions, renovations are usually small enough and will not necessitate extensive job orders. Even so, having a list of contractors to contact for your service needs is crucial. A good Project Manager would have a book composed of different contractors that they have used in the past and completely rely on. If this is not the case, seeking friend referrals is always a good way of finding a new contractor.

Step 4: Noting the Schedule and Cost of the Job

Knowing the extent of the job that needs to be covered makes it easier for you to consult contractors on the task. You have the option of asking contractors directly for an estimate in cost, when they can start and when they can finish the job. This lends beautifully to the Scheduling process as you create program that plans the project from start to finish. The stage also allows PM's to make comparisons and find out which contractors are capable of meeting their specific needs. Don't forget about the terms of the contract and the payment procedure for a completed job.

Step 5: Execution and Monitoring

Once the tasks have been defined and contractors hired, the next step is to oversee the execution of the renovation. A good Project Manager would keep the lines of communication open for all the head contractors in the project. Doing so would make it easier for them to monitor progress and take note of it in their master plan.

Step 6: Assess and Adjust

Lastly, the Manager should routinely check the job being made and adjust their schedule or budget accordingly. Use your contract with the contractor to compare whether the agreed upon cost and schedule are being met. Since Residential Renovation follows a sequence of events, a late completion for part A means that part B will also be behind schedule. A good Project Manager would take this into account and adjust the plan accordingly to ensure that the quality of the project is unaffected.

A well-planned and executed home renovation guarantees the quality of the finished product for the homeowner. Not only that, but by using the guide offered above, you will be able to minimize the possible costs attached to the project. Ideally, a Project Manager for residential renovation should have a partner who double checks the system to ensure accuracy.

Chapter 19: Common Issues Encountered in Construction Project Management

Chapter Objectives:

**Construction Related Problems Encountered in Construction Project Management
** Non-construction Related Problems Encountered in Construction Project Management

There are a number of issues that seek to challenge construction projects, these problems may have just recently been introduced into the construction industry, and still others have already been encountered by individuals involved in this business, from as early as centuries ago. A large number of these problems come as a direct consequence of operations conducted during construction; others are results of collateral damages due to minor processes.

As already previously emphasized, it is the responsibility of the Project Manager to see to it that issues during construction are mitigated before they are even given the chance to escalate and worsen. The Project Manager must be quick about this resolution so as not to compromise the progress of the construction project. The construction cannot afford to waste its time and resources to irrelevant issues.

Examples of construction issues that may threaten to delay and compromise the construction include considerations of the personnel safety, workforce, the time restraint and the varying quality of the work in construction industry itself.

On the one hand, examples of issues that are not at all related to the construction proper include government and environmental regulations, legal issues, and socio-political demands.

Construction Related Problems Encountered in Construction Project Management

1. Personnel Safety – Construction in its inherent nature is a highly dangerous job, with greater tendencies for exposures to hazardous situations. The number of accidents that happen to workers in the construction site remain high every year and continue to cause awfully huge burdens in the construction industry. These burdens weigh far gravely because the losses are in terms of human injury and even death and not in financial losses alone.

In the event that an accident happens to a builder while working in a construction site, construction cost would surely be increased by the medical compensation and insurance recompense as well as the cost to train a new employee and clean up and repair of damaged tool or equipment, the production stalled due to decrease in the number of human work force and delays due to time required for repairs and the completion date of the project possibly postponed at a later date because of failure to meet the demands of the contract. These are the disadvantages that the project faces. However, when compared with the indirect costs that the unfortunate employee suffered, these disadvantages shy from his or her ill circumstance. The individual had to face and deal with the following due to the injury: loss of income earnings for the family, compromised quality of life, and decreased chances of landing another job.

The Project Manager must therefore make it his or her prime objective to ensure safety for personnel within the perimeters of the construction site. It is after all his legal, ethical and moral obligation, it is always included as a demand in the contract, focusing on it would avoid financial problems due to accidents, and complying on established rules and laws for personnel safety in the workplace would provide the company good image and reputation to the public.

149

It is unlawful for any management to subject their employees to unsafe places to work at and violation of this law can result to dire consequences.

2. Workforce – People are and will always be the greatest asset of any industry. In the case of construction projects, the quality of the projects depends heavily on the mental capacity and skills of the people designing plans and accomplishing the work at hand. The essential and distinguishing attribute of the people comprising a company is what makes it unique and sets it apart from all the other companies. It is always to the advantage of the company to hire capable and highly skillful people into their work force.

Unfortunately, hiring a significant number of very skilled workers who have become expert in their fields is becoming more and more difficult. The factors that contribute to this problem involve the dogma that working in the construction industry lacks glamour and class. The construction industry is not exactly the most appealing field to work in for a majority of the professionals, and least of all to recently graduate young professionals. Advancements in technology as well as the rapid growth of other industries have shooed the youth of today from the traditional construction industry.

In order to get our youth attracted to the construction industry once again, it is important that the government team up with public sectors to expose students to the joys and benefits a career in the construction industry offers. They have very good chances to be the ones spearheading these constructions and designing projects. We just have to inspire the masses once again and direct their interest back to this industry.

3. Time Restraint – Time is gold, this cliché has never been as true to any other industry as it is in the construction world. Owners feel money slip from their hands the moment they stop receiving a return to their investment, that instant when they feel their clients are moving further away from them, whenever they spend more on stretched interest payments, and whenever they don't gain profit in all their marketing ventures.

Users on the other hand lose money whenever construction is delayed and the facilities they use operate at an efficiency rate that is way below the optimal standard.

Constructors then lose money when instead of earning they release cash to pay for liquidated damages in the construction process, the delay in the project completion has maximized the project budget to its limit and holds him or her from acquiring new bids, and the delay would mean bad business thus lowered chances of acquiring new bids due to tainted reputation.

The best way to deal with this issue is to practice superior scheduling, planning and control. These qualities are critical recipes to a successful career in the construction industry. Good scheduling skills, being proactive and alert and quick to reacting to unexpected emergencies are essential qualities that one should have in order to avoid or mitigate the negative impacts of time lost or restrained. Never let time work against you, instead allow time to work for your advantage.

4. Nature of the Work in Construction – Construction is a neatly organized collection of mutually dependent activities. The essential nature of construction is characterized by disorder, unpredictability and constant pressures brought by time, budget and resource constraint.

To work in the construction industry means to be subjected to only to seasonal work, sometimes you get hired and at times you do not. You never get the 9-5 job, instead you work based on contracts. Every project you choose to undertake is unique in every way and the progression of its completion is very unpredictable. Your work place is not always the same and often times the construction site where you will be working are situated in far flung areas. The possibility of having the unexpected happen is almost close to a hundred per cent.

Success is heavily dependent on the character and caliber of the people comprising the project team. The work is not conducted in controlled conditions and can be greatly affected by weather and other environmental conditions.

With all these variability and unpredictability of the construction industry, one can readily see how things could easily go wrong in this kind of work environment. There will be times when the weather will never agree with you and the schedule you have laid out for the project. Being an industry that is heavily reliant on the characters involved in it, problems, misunderstandings and interpersonal issues are soon to arise. Also, the problem of being a contractual job does not provide the best encouragement in being a stable source of monetary resource, especially if you are still in the early stages of your career.

Non-construction Related Problems Encountered in Construction Project Management

1. Government Regulation – These comprises the construction codes as well as the licensing requirements that the government has imposed on builders and construction managers. Building codes and licenses continue to increase as time progresses but seldom do they decrease the number of these requirements. There are local building codes on top of national and international codes. There are licensing requirements as well and all these may limit construction designs.

2. Environmental Issues – Ever since the rise of the green revolution, laws and prohibitions that has something to do with protection of the environment has been on the constant rise. Many environmental activists and supporters have been actively working on adding more restrictions to the list of things Project Managers must consider. These regulations designed to ensure public health protect the environment have become more strict than ever and Project Managers must be extremely careful to abide by these regulations or else risk the delay of the project, or worse, its termination, the disqualification from prospective work opportunities in the future, a number of penal fees and civil action and criminal prosecution.

These environmental concerns include the possible impact of construction to the environment such as soil erosion, the leakage of storage tanks and toxic wastes, improper disposal of hazardous waste, dust control, asbestos and lead exposures. The Project Manager should be updated and aware of all these environmental issues before proceeding with construction to avoid project delay and possible disputes against environmental organization supporters.

3. Legal Issues – the construction industry probably ranks high on the list of industries with the greatest risks from legal issues. From the conferment of the contract to start the construction, contractors and clients must first hand seek the support of legal action in order to bind their agreement. At times this contractual nature of the agreement and of the entire business itself leads to disputes and claims.

A claim is a petition expressed by the contractor to obtain additional time extension or compensation for events that are way out of the control of the contractor. With this claim, the contractor must be able to establish a form of entitlement and quantitate and breakdown the related damages incurred. It is important that the claim be presented and filed the moment a situation like this is detected. The sudden modification or alteration to the scope of the project, as well as change in site conditions can be used as grounds for a claim. Claims can also be in the form of extra work, delay or disruption, defective design, acceleration, interference and or impossible performance demand.

The parties involved should work in the least adverse of methods to resolve disputes and settle claims. Both parties should with all patience consider that to resolve the issue before they proceed to becoming legal actions in court would be the most reasonable and less costly course of action. There has been Alternative Dispute Resolution (ADR) for these cases and the practice of these actions have manifested considerable success.

Claims should be avoided in general and the best way to be able to avoid these nasty proceedings during the course of construction of the project is to practice good administrative operations. The communication between the project team, the client and the Project Manager should always be of complete, open and honest communication. It is also in these conflicts that the ability to apply quick troubleshooting to avoid escalation of the problem could prove to be very useful.

4. Socio-Political Pressures – Political pressures along with the community's involvement have been more involved in the matters of the construction industry now more than ever. Pressures have been seen to arise from owners of adjacent properties which include existing residences, businesses, and institutions that are next to the infrastructure to be constructed.

Community groups now have greater input into the design and construction of public works projects, while on the other hand greater impact on the land use and planning process of private constructions. Citizen advisory boards have been utilized to include the community's involvement in the initiation of the project, its design and construction. The increase in the number of stakeholders in construction projects does very little to helping reduce the complexity of the problem.

Chapter 20: Finding Solutions to these Issues Encountered in Construction Project Management

Chapter Objective:

**To understand how Project Managers should Deal with these Issues Encountered during Construction

The modern day Project Manager confronts a number challenges owing to the myriad of problems presented by many sources. These problems obviously have an impact on the success of the project. It is therefore, necessary that the Project Managers demonstrate the strongest ability to recognize the risk and implications of these problems. The Project Manager must be able to quickly and proactively manage these challenges to prevent compromising the success of the project.

Excellent and well capable Project Managers are able to see through these obstacles and navigate through them with little or no negative consequences. These Project Managers should transform risks into opportunities to finish through a construction project with as little downfalls as possible.

Conclusion

With time in consideration, construction project management can be a daunting experience. For one, a Project Manager is on field most of the time. Two, there is still a challenge associated with dealing with a Project Manager or workers that are of the opposite sex. Three, the entire construction process depends on the client's budget. And fourth, there are standards that need to be met. However, for Project Managers, their experience on the field is a great source of learning. If you're about to become a Project Manager for residential construction (or any type of construction for that matter), these simple tips will help you.

- Get involved early especially in the Planning Phase

- Involve all stakeholders and the client

- Have a clear scope of the project and set priorities

- Set realistic expectations and estimates

- Ensure that everyone involved in the construction project know their responsibilities and accountabilities

- Encourage communication among the project members

- Recognize milestones

- Know when to escalate an issue

- Make sure that you update everyone in the team about milestones, changes, and challenges

- Know how to communicated negative news

- Use positive scripting

- Always be on your feet

- Exert your authority in a respectable manner

- Always be fair

Above all, approach every project with a degree of enthusiasm regardless of the environmental or your personal circumstances. It's vital, for the sake of the client that your enthusiasm is there because this will help the entire workforce that work under you to approach the job with equal enthusiasm.

Thank you again for purchasing this book. I hope that you have learned a lot about residential construction in general. The next step for you is to integrate the different concepts discussed as you try to assume your role as a Project Manager. Remember that anyone can be a Project Manager as long as he is flexible enough to "know the trade" and to learn. In the end, it's your own house or residential building you're helping to build.

Finally, if you enjoyed this book, please take the time to share your thoughts and post a review on Amazon. We do our best to reach out to readers and provide the best value we can. Your positive review will help us achieve that. It'd be greatly appreciated!

Thank you and good luck!

Made in the USA
San Bernardino, CA
11 February 2016